THE ATLANTIC CRITICAL STUDIES

JANE AUSTEN'S
Pride and Prejudice

Jibesh Bhattacharyya

ATLANTIC®
PUBLISHERS & DISTRIBUTORS

Published by

ATLANTIC®

PUBLISHERS & DISTRIBUTORS

B-2, Vishal Enclave, Opp. Rajouri Garden,
New Delhi-110027
Phones : 25413460, 25429987, 25466842

Sales Office
7/22, Ansari Road, Darya Ganj,
New Delhi-110002
Phones : 23273880, 23275880, 23280451
Fax : 91-11-23285873
web : www.atlanticbooks.com
e-mail : info@atlanticbooks.com

ISBN 81-269-0549-2

Printed in India
at Nice Printing Press, Delhi

Preface

Jane Austen, a novelist, writing two centuries ago from now, is popular even today and her popularity has been increasing with the passage of time. She is best known for her six novels of which *Pride and Prejudice* is one. *Pride and Prejudice* is considered by many her masterpiece. It is really a wonder that a novelist whose works bear an unmistakable stamp of her time and society should find appreciative and enthusiastic readers among all classes of people in a totally different age.

Every work of literature reflects the author's views, tastes and temperaments. Hence, a proper appreciation of a work of literature requires a knowledge of the writer's life and background. With this aim in view a brief account of Jane Austen's life and work and the society in which she lived, has been given.

The novel has a large number of characters and it refers to a large number of places. So, it sometimes becomes difficult for the readers to follow the narrative, as it is not always possible to remember the relations among the different characters and their individual identities. The various places mentioned in the novel may also create some confusion about their locations and identities. Hence, a list of such persons and places along with their identities has been given as an aid to an uninterrupted reading of the novel.

In order to stimulate interest of the readers in the novel, a brief synopsis and a chapter-wise summary along with a critical analysis of the novel are provided at the beginning, so that armed with these the readers may explore the novel without feeling any confusion or difficulty. This study also makes a critical survey of the different aspects of the novel for its proper comprehension by the discerning readers and students of literature.

A select bibliography is also provided for those who want to make further studies and know the author better. The novel has been written mostly in the form of dialogues and letters and Jane Austen has used words generally employed in speech. To a foreign reader, particularly, many such words may appear unknown and difficult. So, a brief glossary has been provided at the end to help overcome this difficulty. It is expected that a perusal of this critical study and the novel itself will induce the readers to read the other novels of this distinguished woman novelist.

JIBESH BHATTACHARYYA

Contents

	Preface	*iii*
	Introduction	*vii*
1.	Life and Works of Jane Austen	1
2.	Characters and Places	5
3.	A Brief Synopsis of the Novel	17
4.	A Critical Analysis of the Novel	19
5.	The Title of the Novel: Its Significance	65
6.	*Pride and Prejudice*: A Novel of Manners	69
7.	Treatment of the Theme of Money and Marriage	74
8.	Irony and Humour in *Pride and Prejudice*	80
9.	The Plot-Structure	85
10.	Narrative Technique	91
11.	Art of Characterization	94
12.	Character-Sketches	103
	Major Characters	
	Mr Fitzwilliam Darcy	103
	Mr Charles Bingley	106
	Elizabeth Bennet	107
	Jane Bennet	110

Minor Characters

Mr Bennet 112
Mr Collins 114
Mr Wickham 116
Mr Gardiner 119
Mrs Bennet 120
Miss Caroline Bingley 122
Charlotte Lucas 124
Lady Catherine de Bourgh 125
Lydia Bennet 126
Mary Bennet 128
Catherine Bennet (Kitty) 129

13. Jane Austen's Moralistic Outlook 130

14. Jane Austen's Style 133

15. Significance of the Opening Chapter of *Pride and Prejudice* 136

16. The Narrow World of Jane Austen 138

17. A Summing-up 140

18. Critical Reception of the Novel 144

Some Important Questions 149

A Select Bibliography 152

A Brief Glossary 156

Index 163

Introduction

Jane Austen was born at a time when England was torn by wars. On the one hand there was war between Britain and her colonies in America leading to the latter's Independence and there was war between Britain and France known as the Napoleonic wars, on the other. There was also rebellion in Ireland in 1798. Britain was also engaged in war with India for extending her dominion. Moreover, agricultural Britain was fast changing into industrial Britain. Society was then divided into the land-owning aristocracy, the prosperous businessmen, and the poor labourers and workers who were mercilessly exploited by their rich masters. But the peculiarity about Jane Austen is that she remained almost quite unaffected by all these important political, social and economic developments. She was a country girl and remained a country girl all through, although she lived at Bath for some time and made trips to some places in South England. The important historical and political events perhaps did not interest her. Hence she avoided details of contemporary references in her novels. Wars and revolutions were things which did not touch the lives of the common people who were attracted more by such events of universal interest such as love, courtship, marriage, jealousy, social festivities and the like. Jane Austen mentions war briefly in *Pride and Prejudice*, but she uses it only as a device to introduce Wickham. Rightly has Thomas Hardy said: "Yet this [common pursuits of ordinary people, like working in the field or love-making] will go onward the same/Though Dynasties pass" (*In Time of 'The Breaking of Nations'*). Hence, Jane Austen dealt with those incidents which concern individual and society and with those persons whom she knew intimately — the upper middle-class communities containing persons, soldiers and minor aristocracy. The avoidance of detailed contemporary references to important historical and political events made her novels timeless and universal. She writes only of those things in life, which are important to her and the society she lives in. These are family life, courtship, marriage, meetings, the relationships that make up any community.

In Jane Austen's time a gentleman was a man of landed property and was almost an idler having to do nothing for the maintenance of an aristocratic living. The church was a great source of his income, as the aristocracy held most of the best benefices in their hands and sold them as a regular source of income. The various rituals of the church, however, were carried on by ill-paid curates who were never regarded as gentlemen. Jane Austen's father was the owner of a number of church-living. His uncle bought him the rectory of Deane in Hampshire. The adjoining rectory of Steventon was gifted to him by one Mr Knight, a distant relation. The poor curates often married waiting maids and the squires being often their patrons, they were obliged to be very humble and obsequious to those squires. There were also the prosperous businessmen and workers and labourers. But they had little social interactions with the land-owner class. For, they were considered socially inferior by the landed gentry. Even within a class a distinction was maintained according to the amount of wealth a person possessed and alliances took place only within a class. Girls of marriageable age of aristocratic families were introduced to the King and the Queen at the Royal court, while a special ball was arranged for those belonging to families of a lower level, to declare that suitors could pay court to them. Accomplishments rather than learning were considered more important for girls. Such was the condition of the society in which Jane Austen grew up and a reflection of this society is found in her novels.

Jane Austen was more an Augustan than a Romanticist. Rightly has F.E. Pierce in his *Currents and Eddies in the English Romantic Generation* (1918) observed that the mind of Jane Austen was 'femininely Augustan.' The greater part of her life belonged to the eighteenth century. She was twenty-five at the turn of the century. Hence, her beliefs, opinions, attitudes and nature which had already been formed were based on the traditions and the conventions of the eighteenth century. She stands in conspicuous contrast with the Romantic age to which most of her novels belong. The nineteenth century was an age of turbulent thinking. The French Revolution had totally upset the traditional values. Sir Walter Scott and Lord Byron created a distinct world of romanticism while Wordsworth and Shelley added a note of mysticism to it. But neither the wars and revolutions of the outer world of events nor the romanticism and mysticism of the inner world of thought affected her the least. Besides, she was not sentimental. She, unlike the romantic writers of her time, did not turn to Nature for its literal or symbolical implications. She loved Nature like any sensitive observer, but never made a religion of it. She was more interested in the people of her class, people whom she knew intimately. And it will be quite proper to study her as a writer of fiction in the context of the eighteenth century. "Her affinities were with Pope and the Johnson of *The Lives of the Poets,*" observes Walter Allen (*The English Novel*, 1954). Of course, she had more of Addison, Goldsmith and Fanny Burney in her than of Fielding, Sterne or Mrs Ann Radcliffe.

Jane Austen was a realist. In the manipulation of characters and events she left much less to chance than Fielding did. In her novels she brought together the village-folk and their visitors at the dinner party and the ball as naturally as they would meet in real life. Yet it would be misinterpreting her art to think that she was only transcribing actual experiences. What she really did was to build up scenes in her imagination taking details from her personal experiences. There was precisely that selection and re-combination and heightening of incident and character that distinguish the comedy of manners from real life. Besides, Jane Austen was particularly careful regarding dates and places. She would not trust upon hearsay but wanted to have first-hand knowledge before using them in her fiction. The curious might discover many points of contact between her writing and her observation or her reading. No discerning reader would fail to observe the restraint that Jane Austen had voluntarily imposed on herself. Her world was limited geographically, socially and even morally. Her characters never moved out of their country. A visit to Bath was perhaps their sole luxury. The characters were all from the upper middle classes. The leaders of fashion, the aristocratic class and the lower classes — the peasants, the rustics — were absent from her novels. We do not see the extremes of love and hate, righteousness and evil in her novels. She kept her eyes fixed upon the manners of a small circle of country gentlefolk who seemed to have nothing to do but to pay calls, enjoy picnics and walks, drive out, talk and dance. She never used her characters as vehicles for ethical or metaphysical tenets. Thus, conscious of the social reality, a spirit of discipline, a lucid outline and a traditional basis made her a typical Augustan rather than a Romanticist. But in her profound sensibilities and ability to realize the depth of such strong emotions as love and hatred, she imbibed the characteristics of her age. Thus she seemed to have a fusion of the two spirits — the classical and the romantic.

Jane Austen's novels can be viewed from three different angles. The first is purely local. Her novels seem to present a picture-gallery presenting the country life of the upper middle-class in Southern England towards the end of the eighteenth century. Secondly, her novels may be taken, in a way, as an allegorical representation of the various human qualities like sense, sensibilities, pride, prejudice etc. The third is the ironic viewpoint. The various situations, incidents and the characters as presented in her novels imply something more than what the eye can see. They have ironic overtones. Hence, a superficial reading of her novels will fail to satisfy a reader. Her novels are too complex to allow a mere didactic interpretation and too serious to be dismissed as simply light-hearted.

As the novels of Jane Austen are based on the novelist's personal experience, her characters are the most living. The characters are presented to us in such a manner as to make us know them intimately, so that when a crisis arrives they act as we expect them to act. Again, the plots of her novels are so strongly structured that it becomes almost impossible to isolate even the subsidiary characters. Jane Austen's men and women are seen as having a thousand facets. But she never depicted them herself. They were introduced through dialogue and action and not by any comment or interpretation of their creator. Jane Austen was concerned with two aspects of her rural personages: their attention to social duties and their interest in matrimony. And it is on her power of observation that she depended for the supply of her material for the novels. Her strength lay in her concentration upon a limited world and in portraying its every detail.

It is easy to notice a deliberate limitation, a narrowness of range in Jane Austen's choice of subject-matter. But out of this limited range she can develop themes of the broadest significance. It is her moral complexity that enlivens her themes. She does not vehemently renounce the world which she finds coarse and vicious. She can neither abandon the world nor wholly reject its standards. She has a kind tolerant attitude to this world. To her men and women appear silly but kind; wicked, vain, pretentious, stupid, yet attractive; deeply human and capable of love.

In pure technical excellence the novels of Jane Austen are unsurpassed. In the construction of plot, in the development of character and in the artistic display of dramatic situations Jane Austen ranks among the great masters of fiction. She has a kindly tolerance of the manifold follies of life and this makes her take a humorous view of life. And it is in *Pride and Prejudice* that her humour finds full scope for its play.

The style of Jane Austen's novels is clear, direct and slightly tinged with irony. Her spirit reflected gaiety and every page of her novels vibrated with her level-headed good sense and wholesome wit. The lucidity and vitality of her ironic wit might remind one of Congreve's comedies. Jane Austen's preference for the dramatic method involved a severe economy in the use of description. And this technique reached its perfection in *Pride and Prejudice*.

1

Life and Works of Jane Austen

On the 15th of December 1775, the year of American Revolution, was born in the quiet atmosphere of Steventon Parsonage, Hampshire, South England, the seventh child of the Rector of the Parsonage, Reverend George Austen, and Cassandra Leigh Austen. It was a girl child christened Jane who was to become a leading novelist of the first half of the nineteenth century. She did for the English novel what the poets of the period did for English poetry. She made a harmonious blend of her keen personal observation of the realities of a particular section of English life and her fine sensibilities.

Out of the eight children of her parents Jane Austen had one sister and six brothers. Jane Austen was two years younger than her sister Cassandra, named after her mother. The brothers and sisters were very fond of one another and the two sisters enjoyed the greatest affection of their parents. The two sisters Cassandra and Jane had their early education from Mrs. Cawley of Oxford and later at the Abbey School at Reading. Her two brothers Francis and Charles entered The Royal Naval Academy and became admirals. Another brother Henry who became a partner in a banking firm in London helped his sister Jane in her business arrangements with her publishers, later on. Edward, another brother, was adopted by a rich relation and he settled in Godmersham in Kent. His sisters visited him frequently there and almost always did so singly as one of them was needed at home to do the household chores. On such occasions the two sisters wrote to each other regularly and the letters not only reveal the hearts of the two young girls but also present the similarity that existed between them. These letters give us a vivid picture of the private life of Jane Austen. We learn that she served in the family kitchen, did a lot of needle and embroidery work, played, sang and sketched. She also entertained the visitors when any arrived at their house. She regularly went to church on Sundays and often helped the poor and the needy. She read a good deal as one of the few kinds of entertainment available at Steventon where she passed the first twenty-five years of her life. She was acquainted with a number of eighteenth-century fictions, particularly with those of Frances (Fanny) Burney and Mrs Ann Radcliffe. She must have read most of the works of Dr Johnson who influenced her style to a great extent. She must have read also the novels of Richardson and Maria Edgeworth and the poems of Cowper and Crabbe, as the influence of these writers is quite distinct in her works. She, however, felt a great delight when she took part in balls. In many a letter she writes of her delight in the terpsichorean engagements and of her interest in her dance partners. It is, therefore, not difficult to understand why most of the heroines of Jane Austen's novels are fond of the ball and why all the romance in them starts from society ball dances.

One may presume that Jane Austen had not willingly accepted a life of celibacy. And meeting of men, mutual assessment of suitability, courtship and marriage must have seemed to her things of importance and perhaps she had her wish-fulfilment by making these the key topics in her novels. She never rushed into any financially sound but emotionally unworthy marriage. She, however, had a romance with a young man when she and the members of her family moved to Bath in 1801, when her father retired from holy orders having installed his eldest son James in his place. She was on the point of engagement when the young man was killed in a tragic accident. Later, one Harris Bigg-Wither proposed to her and she accepted the proposal, but by the next morning she discovered that she did not love him and so she broke off the engagement. In this connection the following statement of Jane Austen in the unfinished sketch of her novel, *The Watsons* (1804), is interesting to note :

> To be so bent on marriage — to pursue a man merely for the sake of situation — is a sort of thing that shocks me! I cannot understand it. Poverty is a great evil, but, to a woman of education and feeling, it ought not, it cannot be the greatest — I would rather be a Teacher at a school than marry a man I did not like.

Both Jane and her sister Cassandra did not marry and the life of a spinster in the early nineteenth-century England was greatly hazardous and an old maid was looked upon as a freak and was either laughed at or condemned. But, luckily for the Austen sisters, they did not have to face any ignominy for their spinsterhood, rather they were loved by all because of the instinctive excellence of their character. It is only by imposing on herself the most severe self-discipline, by alert attention to the comfort of other people, by sympathizing with, listening to and running errands for others was Jane Austen able to hold the sympathy and consideration of her community. And in writing her novels, which was a pursuit of pleasure to her, she received great considerations from her relations.

Jane Austen began writing very early in life. She greatly loved her literary work and deeply enjoyed writing. She wrote regularly and at a great speed. She started writing when she was just a girl of twelve. Her early writings were in manuscripts which she entitled, 'Volume the First,' 'Volume the Second' and 'Volume the Third' and in them we may find the seeds of her six novels which she wrote later. By 1793 she has completed *Love and Friendship* and by 1796 she had written *Lady Susan* and *Elinor and Marianne* (the first version of *Sense and Sensibility*) in the Richardsonian epistolary form. She had already started writing *First Impressions* which was later revised as *Pride and Prejudice*. This was taken to a publisher by her father who even offered to pay the cost of publication, himself, but it was rejected. Later in 1813 the revised version entitled *Pride and Prejudice* was published and it came to be considered her *chef d'oeuvre*. Before that in November 1811 she published *Sense and Sensibility*, the revised version of *Elinor and Marianne*, at her own expense.

Jane Austen's father died in 1805 when she along with her mother and sister shifted to Southampton. Four years later, in 1809, being invited by one of her brothers, she left Southampton with her mother and sister to live with him at Chawton near Winchester in the county of Hampshire. Life at Chawton was quite happy for them amidst the members of the younger generation. It was during this period of happiness of her life that Jane Austen turned again to novel writing. Now appeared in close succession *Mansfield Park* (1814) and *Emma* (1815). *Northanger Abbey* (the revised version of *Lady Susan* composed between 1792 and 1796) and *Persuasion* (composed in 1815-16) only saw the light of the day posthumously in 1818. *Lady Susan* (the original version of *Northanger Abbey*) and a fragment, *The Watsons* (composed in 1804) were published in *A Memoir of Jane Austen* by J.E. Austen-Leigh later in 1870.

By 1816 the health of Jane Austen began to fail. She heroically struggled against the incurable disease of consumption which had gradually seized hold of her. She even began a new novel *Sandition* in 1817. In May that year she was taken to Winchester by her sister for better medical attention. There in a rented house she quietly breathed her last two months later in the early morning of 18th July 1817 leaving her last work incomplete. She was buried in Winchester Cathedral in as simple and serene a manner in which she passed her life.

Jane Austen had doubts about how the public would receive her novels and also had little hope of their publication. She, however, wrote for the sheer pleasure of writing and tried to make her work as perfect as she could, which was obvious from the several revisions she had made of her novels. She had little contact with the great writers of the day and she never aspired after name and fame. Thus, when Mr Clarke, the librarian of Carlton House, suggested her to dedicate her next novel to the Prince Regent who greatly appreciated her novels, she offered her novel *Emma* published in December 1815, to the Prince. But she never longed for any princely favour and she was not ready to go out of her way to please the Prince. She did not get her due recognition from the reading public of her time, yet discerning readers like Sir Walter Scott and Robert Southey admired her work greatly.

2

Characters and Places

As *Pride and Prejudice* has a large number of characters and as it refers to a large number of places, it becomes rather difficult for a reader to remember them and this will mar his/her enjoyment of the novel. Hence, a list of characters with their identities and a list of places with their locations are now provided.

The Characters

The Male Characters :

Bennet, Mr	:	The head of the Bennet family and father of Elizabeth and her four sisters.
Bingley, Charles	:	He belongs to a respectable family in the north of England, rents Netherfield House in the neighbourhood of the Bennet family, loves and finally marries Jane, the eldest sister of the Bennet family.
Carter, Captain	:	He belongs to the regiment of Colonel Forster.
Chamberlayne	:	An acquaintance of Lydia Bennet and the Forsters.
Collins, William	:	A cousin of Mr Bennet whose estate is entailed, in default of a male heir, to him. He is the Rector of Hunsford Parsonage under the patronage of Lady Catherine de Bourgh. He married Charlotte Lucas. He is twenty-five.

Darcy, Fitzwilliam	:	He is the son of Lady Anne Darcy and nephew of Lady Catherine de Bourgh. He is the hero of the novel. He is 28 years old and the owner of the Pemberley Estate with an annual income of £10,000. His 'pride' results in 'prejudice' of Elizabeth whom he finally marries.
Dawson	:	Coachman of Lady Catherine de Bourgh.
Denny	:	He belongs to Colonel Forster's regiment. He helps Wickham to get into that regiment and later informs Colonel Forster about Wickham's real intention in eloping with Lydia.
Fitzwilliam, Colonel	:	He is the younger son of an Earl who is the brother of Darcy's mother and Lady Catherine de Bourgh. Aged about 30, he is a perfect gentleman and very entertaining.
Forster, Colonel	:	He is the colonel of the regiment staying first at Meryton and then at Brighton. He plays an active role in search of the runaway couple, Wickham and Lydia.
Gardiner, Edward	:	He is the brother of Mrs Bennet. He has a major role in the reconciliation of Lydia and Wickham.
Gouldings, The	:	They are acquaintances of Mrs Bennet living at Haye-Park in the neighbourhood of the Bennets.
Goulding, William	:	In order to reveal her honourable status Lydia contrives to make him see her wedding-ring while driving home from London.

Haggerston	:	He is engaged by Mr Gardiner for making proper settlement in favour of Lydia, as stipulated by Wickham for marrying her.
Hurst, Mr	:	He is the husband of Louisa, the eldest of the two Bingley sisters.
John	:	A servant, recommended by Lady Catherine de Bourgh, to Mrs Collins (Charlotte Lucas) for accompanying Maria Lucas and Elizabeth Bennet on their journey back to London from Hunsford.
Jones, Mr	:	An apothecary of Meryton, who attended on Jane Bennet while she was lying ill at Netherfield House.
Lewis de Bourgh, Sir	:	The deceased husband of Lady Catherine de Bourgh.
Lucas, Sir William	:	He is the head of the Lucas family living in the neighbourhood of the Bennet family at Longbourn. Collins marries his daughter, Charlotte Lucas.
Morris	:	The owner of Netherfield House hired by Mr Bingley.
Nicholls	:	The cook at Netherfield House.
Philips	:	He is the husband of Mrs Bennet's sister. He is an attorney. He visits all the officers of Colonel Forster's regiment.
Pratt	:	An acquaintance of Lydia and the Forsters.
Richard	:	Servant of Philips.
Robinson	:	A participant at Meryton Ball. Bingley tells him that he considers Jane the prettiest of girls.

Stone	:	He is the man to whom Mr Gardiner was called away upon business, just when he was about to start for St. Clement's for marrying Lydia and Wickham. He is probably Wickham's lawyer.
Wickham, George	:	He is the son of the steward of Darcy's father. He is a profligate and villain of the novel. He gets into Colonel Forster's regiment and spreads calumny about Darcy. He elopes with Lydia to London and is finally compelled to marry her.

The Female Characters :

Annesley, Mrs	:	She lives with Miss Darcy in London. She helps to ease the situation tactfully at Pemberley House of Darcy, where Elizabeth and others are invited to dinner.
Bennet, Mrs	:	She is the mother of the five Bennet sisters and sister of Mr Gardiner and Mrs Philips.
Bennet, Catherine (Kitty)	:	She is the fourth daughter of Mr and Mrs Bennet. She is 17. Till the end of the novel she remains unmarried.
Bennet, Elizabeth (Lizzy)	:	She is the second daughter of the Bennet family, aged 20. She is the heroine of the novel. She loves Darcy but keeps away from him out of her 'prejudice' for his 'pride' and is ultimately united with him.
Bennet, Jane	:	She is the eldest of the Bennet sisters, aged 22. She loves Bingley and is finally married to him.

Bennet, Lydia	:	She is the youngest and tallest of the Bennet sisters, aged 15. She elopes with Wickham and is ultimately married to him by the earnest effort of Darcy.
Bennet, Mary	:	She is the third daughter of Mr and Mrs Bennet. She works hard for knowledge and accomplishment. When Jane, Elizabeth and Lydia get married and leave Longbourn permanently, she remains unmarried and stays on with her mother.
Bingley, Miss Caroline	:	She is the unmarried sister of Charles Bingley. Being desirous of winning the rich Darcy for her husband, she becomes instrumental in separating her brother, Charles Bingley, from Jane so that her brother may marry Darcy's sister, Georgiana, and she, Darcy.
Catherine de Bourgh, Lady	:	She is the widow of Sir Lewis de Bourgh, sister of Darcy's mother and Colonel Fitzwilliam's father. She is the owner of Rosings and patron of Collins.
Darcy, Georgiana	:	She is the sister of Darcy. She is a graceful and accomplished girl of 16. With a fortune of £30,000 she is under the joint guardianship of Darcy and Colonel Fitzwilliam.
Darcy, Lady Anne	:	She is the deceased mother of Fitzwilliam Darcy and sister of Lady Catherine de Bourgh and also of Colonel Fitzwilliam's father.

De Bourgh, Miss Anne	:	She is the only child of Lady Catherine de Bourgh and Sir Lewis de Bourgh, and heiress of Rosings.
Forster, Mrs Harriet	:	Lydia claims her to be her close friend to whom she leaves a note on the eve of her elopement with Wickham mentioning their intended marriage at Gretna Green on the border of South Scotland.
Gardiner, Mrs	:	Wife of Mr Edward Gardiner, the brother of Mrs Bennet.
Harriet	:	A female acquaintance of Lydia and the Forsters.
Hill, Mrs	:	The cook of the Bennets.
Hurst, Mrs Louisa	:	The wife of Mr Hurst and elder sister of Caroline Bingley.
Jenkinson, Mrs	:	Governess of Miss de Bourgh, daughter of Lady Catherine de Bourgh.
King, Miss	:	A participant in the Meryton ball and object of interest of Wickham because of her fortune of £10,000.
Long, Mrs	:	A neighbour of Mrs Bennet.
Lucas, Charlotte	:	She is the eldest of the Lucas daughters and a friend of Elizabeth Bennet. When Collins proposes to her, after being rejected by Elizabeth, she at once accepts the proposal and marries him for security.
Lucas, Lady	:	Wife of Sir William Lucas, mother of Charlotte Lucas and a friend of Mrs Bennet.
Lucas, Maria	:	She is the second daughter of the Lucas family and sister of Charlotte Lucas. She accompanies Elizabeth

		Bennet to Hunsford Parsonage when Elizabeth goes there to meet her friend Charlotte Lucas after Charlotte's marriage with Collins.
Metcalfe, Lady	:	An acquaintance of Lady Catherine de Bourgh.
Nicholls, Mrs	:	She is the wife of the cook at Netherfield House. She gives Mrs Philips, sister of Mrs Bennet, the news that Mr Bingley is expected to arrive at Netherfield House for the second time.
Pen	:	A female acquaintance of Lydia and the Forsters.
Philips, Mrs	:	She is the wife of Mr Philips and sister of Mrs Bennet and Mr Gardiner.
Pope, Miss	:	She is in the employ of Lady Metcalfe on the recommendation of Lady Catherine de Bourgh.
Reynolds, Mrs	:	She is the housekeeper of Mr Darcy's Pemberley House and shows Elizabeth and her aunt round the house when they come to visit the house on invitation.
Sally	:	A domestic of Mr Forster.
Sarah	:	A domestic of the Bennets.
Watson, Miss	:	Colonel Forster and Captain Carter often visit her at Meryton.
Webb, The Misses	:	Lady Catherine de Bourgh often cites the example of the Misses Web while speaking of playing and singing.
Younge, Mrs	:	She is a wicked woman living in London with Miss Darcy and arranges the intended elopement

of Miss Darcy with Wickham from Ramsgate. Later, being bribed, she reveals to Darcy the address of Wickham and Lydia after the two have eloped.

The Places — Their Location

Ashworth	:	A place ten miles away from Longbourn House of the Bennets.
Bakewell	:	A place en route to Pemberley.
Barnet	:	A place on the way to Hertfordshire from Brighton through Epsom and Clapham.
Barnet Road	:	A road going to Scotland.
Bell, The	:	The name of an inn in Bromley.
Birmingham	:	A notable place on the way to Derbyshire from Longbourn.
Blenheim	:	A notable place on the route from Longbourn to Derbyshire.
Brighton	:	A well-known coastal town in Sussex, south of London.
Bromley	:	A place on the way to London from Hunsford.
Chatsworth	:	It is a famous aristocratic mansion in Derbyshire.
Cheapside	:	A part of London where generally the people of lower classes live, and which is a place of business.
Clapham	:	A town situated in the south of the Thames in central London. It was a village in Jane Austen's day.
Clarke' s Library	:	It is situated in Meryton.
Dovedale	:	It is a beautiful valley in Derbyshire, that forms a part of the Peak district.

Eastbourne	:	A place in the west of Brighton. It is a sea resort.
Edward Street	:	It is in London, where Mrs Younge has taken a large house which she intends to use for letting purposes.
Epsom	:	A town in Surrey in the south of London. It was a health resort in Jane Austen's time.
George, The	:	An inn in a town in Hertfordshire, from where Mr Bennet's carriage takes Elizabeth and Jane home after Elizabeth's visit to Rosings.
Gracechurch Street	:	A street near Cheapside in London, where the Gardiners live. There, in the house of the Gardiners, the two sisters, Jane and Elizabeth, and their friend Maria Lucas stayed for a few days on their way to Longbourn from Rosings.
Gretna Green	:	It is a place on the border of England in Dumfriesshire in South Scotland. Here runaway couples from England could marry with impunity.
Grosvenor Street	:	A street in London, where Mr Hurst, husband of Louisa, the eldest of the Bingley sisters, has a house. It is a very fashionable area in London.
Haye-Park	:	A place in the neighbourhood of Longbourn where the Gouldings lived. Mrs Bennet thought of renting the house there for Lydia after her marriage with Wickham.

Hatfield	:	A place on the way to Hertfordshire from Brighton through Epsom and Clapham.
Hertfordshire	:	It is a county of England on the north of London.
Hunsford	:	It is a parish near Westerham in Kent. The valuable rectory of this parish is gifted to Collins by Lady Catherine.
Hunsford Lane	:	This is a passage that leads to Hunsford Parsonage separating its garden from Rosings Park.
Hunsford Parsonage	:	It is a house adjoining Rosings Park. It is occupied by Collins.
Jones's Shop	:	It is situated at Meryton.
Kenilworth	:	A market town in Warwick, four miles south-west of Coventry.
Kympton	:	A village in Derbyshire, whose benefice is a valuable gift of Darcy.
Lakes, The	:	They refer to the lakes in Westmoreland, Cumberland and Lancashire in England. The area is known as the Lake District and is still a popular spot for tours.
Lambton	:	It is a small market-town in Derbyshire, five miles away from Pemberley.
Little Theatre, The	:	It is in London near the lodgings of Wickham.
Longbourn	:	It is a village in Hertfordshire where the Bennets live. It is a mile away from Meryton, three miles from Netherfield House and twenty-four miles away from London.

Longbourn House	:	It is the residence of the Bennets with a small park.
Lucas Lodge	:	It is a house with a park, situated about a mile from Meryton, occupied by the Lucases.
Matlock	:	A beautiful spot in Derbyshire. It is a watering place.
Meryton	:	It is a market town one mile away from Longbourn House on the way to Netherfield Park.
Netherfield House	:	It is three miles away from Longbourn House on the way to Meryton. This grand house with its park was rented by Mr Bingley.
Netherfield Park	:	The area including Netherfield House and its Park.
Newcastle	:	It is a well-known sea-coast town in Northumberland in the north of England.
Oakham Mount	:	It is in the neighbourhood of Longbourn House.
Peak, The	:	A beautiful spot in Derbyshire.
Pemberley	:	It is in Derbyshire, to the north of Hertfordshire. It is about thirty-six hours' journey from Longbourn by post-chaise. It is Darcy's estate with Pemberley House and the woods.
Pemberley House	:	The house owned by Darcy in the Pemberley estate.
Pemberley Woods	:	It is a beautiful wood in the Pemberley estate and is ten miles in circumference.

Purvis Lodge	:	It is a house in the neighbourhood of Longbourn House. According to Mrs Bennet its attics are dreadful.
Ramsgate	:	It is a coastal town to the south-east of London.
Rosings	:	The residence of Lady Catherine de Bourgh in Kent, near Hunsford Parsonage.
Rosings Park	:	A park of Rosings adjoining Hunsford Lane and Hunsford Parsonage.
Scarborough	:	It is a sea-side town on the east coast of Yorkshire and north-east of Derbyshire.
St. Clements	:	It is a church in the city of London, where Wickham and Lydia are married.
Stoke	:	It is a place near the Longbourn House, where there is a great house which Mrs Bennet is thinking of renting for Lydia after her marriage.
Warwick	:	A county town on the river Avon, eight miles south-west of Coventry in England.

3

A Brief Synopsis of the Novel

The story of the novel *Pride and Prejudice* revolves round the theme of marriage. A middle-class family consisting of the husband, Mr Bennet, his wife, Mrs Bennet, and their five marriageable daughters, Jane, Elizabeth, Mary, Catherine and Lydia, lived in the village of Longbourn in Hertfordshire. Mr Bennet's estate was entailed, in default of a male heir, to his cousin Mr Collins who was the Rector of Hunsford under the patronage of Lady Catherine de Bourgh. Thus, with little fortune to push her daughters in the world, Mrs Bennet was naturally looking forward very anxiously to prospective sons-in-law. One day Charles Bingley, a rich bachelor having a fortune of four thousand a year, came and settled in Netherfield Park near Longbourn, along with his two sisters and his friend Fitzwilliam Darcy, nephew of Lady Catherine de Bourgh. Soon an opportunity came to an eager Mrs Bennet to meet Bingley at a ball, with all her five daughters. Bingley and Jane, the eldest of the Bennet girls, now fell mutually in love. Mr Darcy, who was somewhat vain and highbrow, curtly refused to dance with Elizabeth saying that she was not beautiful enough to tempt him, although in reality he was attracted to her. This aversion of Darcy was intensified when he and the sisters of Bingley, disgusted with the impropriety of Mrs Bennet and her younger daughters, effected the separation of Bingley and Jane. Miss Caroline Bingley's purpose in effecting this separation was that it would brighten her own prospect of marrying Darcy, the owner of the magnificent estate of Pemberley yielding an income of nearly ten thousand pounds a year, with her brother marrying Darcy's sister. Meanwhile Collins proposed to Elizabeth and was brusquely rejected. Collins promptly turned to the sensible, worldly-wise Charlotte Lucas, the eldest daughter of the Lucases, who lived near Longbourn, and married her. Being invited by Charlotte who was a close friend of Elizabeth, the latter went to live with her friend for a few days. There Elizabeth met Darcy who then had been living with his aunt, Lady Catherine de Bourgh who lived in the neighbourhood. Now, strongly attracted to Elizabeth in spite of himself, Darcy proposed to her. But Elizabeth had already learnt how Darcy treated Mr Wickham, a handsome military officer, most unjustly and how he was also responsible for ruining the prospective marriage of her sister Jane to Mr Bingley. So, Elizabeth rejected Darcy's offer most indignantly, giving him the reasons. The very next day Darcy in a letter to Elizabeth successfully cleared himself from the two charges levelled against him. Now, on a trip to the north of England with her uncle and aunt, Mr and Mrs Gardiner, Elizabeth visits Pemberley, Darcy's place in Derbyshire. There they were cordially welcomed by Darcy, and Elizabeth was much influenced by his polished and courteous manner. Meanwhile news reached Elizabeth that Lydia had eloped with Wickham, son of the steward of Darcy's property and an unprincipled adventurer. The shocking part of the news was that the eloped couple could not be traced and that there was little chance of Wickham marrying Lydia. By Darcy's secret aid the fugitives were traced and their marriage was brought about, thereby saving the Bennet family from the inevitable scandal. At this point Bingley arrived at Netherfield with Darcy and his attachment to Jane was renewed, and this led to their engagement. Elizabeth's attitude to Darcy had already been changed. So, when Darcy proposed to Elizabeth now, she readily accepted the proposal in spite of the insolent intervention of Lady Catherine, Darcy's aunt. In due course Jane was married to Bingley and Elizabeth to Darcy. Now only two of the Bennet daughters, Mary and Catherine, remained to be married. Of them Mary with her unattractive manners had little chance of finding a husband. But, Catherine had a fair chance to have a happy future, and under the improving influence of her elder sisters she developed into an accomplished young lady.

4

A Critical Analysis of the Novel

That a single man with a good fortune must be in need of a wife, is a truth universally acknowledged. So, when Mr Bingley, a handsome bachelor with a fortune settles in Netherfield Park, Mrs Bennet of the neighbouring Longbourn with five marriageable daughters urges her husband to visit the newcomer. Mr Bennet teases his wife by pretending his reluctance, although he really wishes to make the visit.

This opening chapter and the opening sentence, in particular, is a unique example of Jane Austen's masterly use of irony. It immediately introduces us to the theme of marriage, to the efforts of mothers to get their daughters married. That marriage often depends on economic consideration is hinted at in this chapter. The irony of the opening sentence is revealed when we find Mrs Bennet needs a single man with a good fortune, Mr Bingley, for any one of her five single daughters. And Mr Bingley is called 'the rightful property' of a young lady. Thus, the young man of fortune is considered the hunted rather than the hunter. From this jumping board Jane Austen leaps into the complexities of human relationships in her novel. We are introduced in this chapter to two important characters, Mr and Mrs Bennet, and we discover how mismatched a pair they are. Mr Bennet is much given to wit and irony and has a sarcastic humour, while Mrs Bennet is a woman of mean understanding, little information and uncertain temper. We also learn that Mr Bennet does not have a very high opinion of either his wife or any one of his daughters, except Elizabeth.

(*Chapter 1*)

Mr Bennet is one of Mr Bingley's earliest callers, but keeps his wife in suspense about the visit and enjoys her apprehension of any other neighbouring woman capturing Mr Bingley. Then as he reveals the pleasing fact of his visit to Mr Bingley, Mrs Bennet becomes enthusiastic in her praise of her husband, and to avoid her effusive gratitude Mr Bennet leaves the room. The mother and the daughters now engage themselves in discussing about Bingley.

This chapter throws further light on the relationship among the members of the Bennet family. It may be considered another introductory chapter, presenting the atmosphere of upper middle-class life, setting the scene for Bingley's arrival and introducing us to the five Bennet sisters. Mr Bennet views with irony all that his wife says or does. He appears to be intellectually superior to his wife and most of his daughters. But his teasing of Mary is not tempered with kindness and tolerance. He is rather cold and unpleasant. The conversation between Mrs Bennet and others reveals some of the social codes and conventions prevalent at the time, as, for example, the time that should be allowed to pass before inviting a new acquaintance to dinner.

(*Chapter* 2)

As Mr Bennet refuses to give any further information about Mr Bingley, Mrs Bennet and her daughters have to remain satisfied with the account of him given by Lady Lucas. Mr Bingley pays a short return visit to the Bennets but declines an offer for dinner. He, however, attends a ball at Meryton, within a fortnight, where he comes with his two sisters, one brother-in-law and a friend, Mr Darcy. Mrs Bennet attends this ball with all her daughters. Mr Bingley takes a particular fancy to Jane, dancing with her twice. Darcy, who is more handsome and richer than Bingley, fails to impress the assembly for his pride and vanity. He does not mix with Meryton society. He dances only with Miss Bingley. When Bingley suggests that Darcy should dance with Elizabeth, Darcy comments that she is 'not handsome enough to tempt me'. This fills the mind of Elizabeth with a deep prejudice against Darcy. Returning home an overjoyed Mrs Bennet bores her husband by giving a detailed account of everything that has happened.

In this chapter almost all the principal characters have been introduced. Here we see the first social meeting between Darcy and Elizabeth. And from their very first meeting their pride and prejudice are established. Thus, this chapter lays the foundation of the conflict presented in the novel. Darcy is presented as conceited and disagreeable. But at the first description Darcy is presented as fine, handsome and noble. This is the real Darcy. Jane Austen has shown how prejudice can present an erring view of a person. For, Darcy may have sufficient reason to remain aloof from the company and appear proud. Elizabeth does not appear here as a romantic heroine. She feels insulted by Darcy's remarks, but at first seems to be amused by it, although she does not forget it. Her prejudice is the result of her wounded pride because of Darcy's remarks. Darcy is proud of his social position and prejudiced against people of lower rank; Elizabeth is proud of her superior intellect and becomes prejudiced against Darcy who fails to recognize her quality.

(*Chapter 3*)

When Jane and Elizabeth are alone, they talk about the ball at Meryton. Jane confides to Elizabeth how much she likes Bingley. She is also delighted with Bingley's sisters. Jane being incapable of seeing ill in anyone, Elizabeth does not give much importance to her opinion, although she admits the merits of Bingley and considers his sisters not much agreeable. Mr Bingley, with a property of about a hundred thousand pounds, is free, frank and accommodating. Mr Darcy is proud, haughty, reserved and aristocratic. Yet, the two are very good friends. They talk a lot about the Meryton assembly. While Bingley is charmed with the whole assembly and particularly with Jane, Darcy does not make much of it, although he makes a qualified approval of Jane. The Bingley sisters, however, admire Jane as a sweet girl.

This chapter presents before us two pairs of contrasting characters who are to play major roles in the novel. They are Jane and Elizabeth, on the one hand, and Bingley and Darcy, on the other. The difference of class and status, so vital to the novel, is carefully established in the attitudes of Darcy and Elizabeth to each other. Jane Austen depends much on dialogue to reveal characters. To Jane the whole world appears as simple and decent as she herself is. Elizabeth is intelligent, realistic and candid in her opinion as we notice by her remarks on the Bingleys. Darcy is almost like Elizabeth in his intelligence, frankness and clear-sightedness. Some good points of Darcy's character are brought out in this chapter, although they are not developed till much later. Elizabeth's critical approach to life and people has been artfully contrasted with the uncritical credulity and easy manners of Jane. The plot receives a slight push forward by the Bingley sisters' favourable opinion of Jane, on which some subsequent incidents are built.

(*Chapter 4*)

On the next morning after the Meryton assembly, Charlotte Lucas, a friend of Elizabeth and daughter of Sir William Lucas, a rich business-man of Meryton, comes to visit the Bennets along with her sisters and a brother. Mrs Bennet is upset that Bingley chose Charlotte as his first dance partner although he danced later twice with Jane. Darcy's comment about Elizabeth is then mentioned and while Mrs Bennet condemns him outright as a proud insolent person, Charlotte defends him on the ground of his wealth and position, supported also by her brother.

In this chapter, pride and prejudice, the central themes of the novel, are juxtaposed explicitly for the first time. This chapter adds to the climate of near desperation among marriageable women against which the whole novel is set. Even dances take on vital significance as signs of affection and love. Darcy's pride is seriously discussed and condemned without any knowledge of his true character, and this is only because a general social prejudice is against him. That Elizabeth's prejudice has its root in her pride is clear in her remark, 'I could easily forgive his pride, if he had not mortified mine'. Through Charlotte and her brother Jane Austen seems to add some clues to warn the reader against forming any hasty opinion about Darcy.

(*Chapter 5*)

The Bennet and the Bingley sisters exchange visits and soon Jane and Mr Bingley become fonder of each other. Jane being reserved will not disclose the feelings of her heart and so Elizabeth feels happy that the good name of their family will not be stained if Jane's love does not culminate in marriage. But Charlotte is of the opinion that in matters of love too much of concealment may sometimes prove to be harmful. She believes in the practicality of marriage as happiness is entirely a matter of chance. Hence, unless a woman reveals herself, her love will never be reciprocated. Meanwhile, Darcy has developed his interest in Elizabeth. At the Lucases' party he watches her closely and notices her big eyes and easy playfulness. He is ready to dance with her, but Elizabeth, remembering the unhappy Meryton episode, refuses to dance with him. This strong-mindedness of Elizabeth attracts Darcy even more. Miss Caroline Bingley, who cherishes hopes to marry Darcy, becomes jealous of Elizabeth.

In this chapter the idea of marriage as a financial and social contract has been presented for the first time. It is, however, ironic that eventually both Charlotte and Elizabeth make financially sound marriages. Not only this; the very rich husband that Elizabeth at first condemns becomes attracted to her. The attitude of Charlotte towards marriage is an indication of her own uncertainty and a preparation for her own action in choosing a husband. Darcy's prejudice against Elizabeth changes in this chapter while Elizabeth's prejudice will take some more time to dissolve. The change in Darcy is not unconvincing, as some critics hold, as, he finds Elizabeth different from other women whom he has so far encountered. The force of her intellect and her independent personality attract him greatly. The presence of Caroline Bingley, a shallow selfish woman, helps Darcy, in a way, to realize the true merit of Elizabeth.

(*Chapter* 6)

Mr Bennet's estate of Longbourn with an annual income of two thousand pounds is entailed, in default of a male heir, on a distant relation. Mrs Bennet, the daughter of an attorney at Meryton, has a sister, Mrs Philips, to whom Catherine and Lydia visit after being motivated by the arrival of a regiment in the town. Mr Bennet is disgusted by his daughters' fondness for the army officers and calls them the silliest girls on earth. Jane receives an invitation to dine and spend a day with the Bingley sisters. Mrs Bennet, anticipating rain, advises Jane to go there on horseback, thinking that the rain and the absence of a carriage will detain her at Netherfield giving her an opportunity to improve her relations with Mr Bingley. As has been expected, Jane arrives at Netherfield wet, and falls ill. Mrs Bennet is delighted that Jane has to remain at Netherfield longer as she has caught cold. On hearing about Jane's illness Elizabeth becomes very worried and walks over to visit her sister and despite Miss Bingley's antagonism, Miss Bingley invites Elizabeth to stay on and look after Jane.

This chapter brings out the silliness of the two youngest Bennet sisters and their mother's lack of good sense. Mr Bennet's attitude towards his two daughters also is made clear. The beginning of this chapter reveals the harsh economic realities of the time. At that time the typical English woman had no economic or legal standing in society. This makes her more dependant on a husband. Mr and Mrs Bennet reveal themselves more in this chapter. Mrs Bennet shows her shallow values and coarseness in approving the flirtations of her daughters. Mr Bennet seems to lack the personality to oppose his wife. This chapter shows Elizabeth's real concern for Jane. Her walk to Netherfield reveals her impetuosity, and the reactions of Caroline Bingley and Darcy to her arrival show their characters quite well. While Miss Bingley is amused to see the muddy and dishevelled Elizabeth, Darcy seems to be embarrassed by her condition.

(*Chapter* 7)

Elizabeth stays in attendance on her sister Jane as her condition has not improved. In her absence the Bingley sisters criticize her as a low and uncultivated person. Mrs Hurst appreciates Jane as a sweet girl but speaks of her low connections. As Jane falls asleep in the evening, Elizabeth goes downstairs to find the party busy playing cards. Elizabeth decides to read rather than play cards. Caroline taunts her for this and turns the talk to Darcy's fine library at Pemberley. She now continues her talk with Mr Darcy on the matter of a lady's real accomplishment. Darcy criticizes the contemporary idea that music and needlework alone are sufficient accomplishments and lays emphasis on the improvement of mind by extensive reading.

The Bingley sisters hotly contest this observation of Darcy and the talk comes to an end when Elizabeth leaves the room and goes to Jane. Jane's condition is worse. So, it is decided to call Mr Jones, the apothecary, the next morning.

This chapter is important for the revelation of characters. It not only allows the romance of Jane and Bingley to develop but also helps Darcy and Elizabeth get to know each other. More areas of compatibility between these two principal characters are brought into view, one of which is reading. Caroline's narrowness and jealousy and Bingley's kind and gentle nature are also revealed in this chapter. Darcy, by his dislike of Miss Bingley's flattery and sarcasm, and by a tacit appreciation of Elizabeth, foreshadows the future development of the plot. Elizabeth shows another facet of her character by her love for her sister Jane and concern for her illness.

(*Chapter 8*)

The next morning Mr Jones as well as Mrs Bennet, who has been sent for, comes to see Jane. Although Jane has improved a little, Mrs Bennet wants her to stay at Netherfield a few more days in the company of Mr Bingley. Mr Jones also advises Jane to have some rest. Bingley is happy that Jane must stay on for a few days. Mrs Bennet becomes an object of fun and mirth to the Bingley sisters because of her stupidity and vulgar vanity in defending the social life in the country. Elizabeth vainly tries to shield her mother and as soon as her mother departs, she hurries upstairs to Jane. Lydia, who has also come with her mother, exacts a promise from Mr Bingley that he will hold a ball. After Mrs Bennet's departure the Bingley sisters and Darcy talk insultingly of the Bennet family.

This chapter brings Darcy and the Bingleys into their closest contact with the Bennets. This contact strengthens Darcy's feeling of superiority which is to cause further problems. This chapter shows Mrs Bennet with all her stupidity, vulgarity and shallowness in the affairs of the world. Elizabeth's comments show her interest in people, although her judgment of the characters of Bingley and Darcy is not altogether correct. Lydia's request to Bingley leads to the crucial Netherfield ball.

(*Chapter 9*)

In the morning Mrs Hurst and Miss Bingley spend some time with Jane and in the evening Elizabeth joins the ladies and others in the drawing room. There Darcy is writing a letter to his sister and Elizabeth engages herself in some needle work. Miss Bingley constantly seeks the attention of Darcy by praising and showering compliments on his handwriting without any results. Darcy criticizes Bingley for his impulsiveness and Elizabeth joins in this discussion and defends Bingley. Bingley turns the conversation by teasing Darcy about his bad moods and soon after the ladies are asked for some music. As Elizabeth refuses to sing, Miss Bingley and Mrs Hurst sing two songs. After the music is over Darcy requests Elizabeth to dance with him, which she curtly refuses. Darcy is not offended but takes the refusal gallantly. Darcy's growing feeling for Elizabeth is now clear to Caroline who begins to tease him on this issue. Next morning Miss Bingley and Mrs Hurst leave Elizabeth alone and want to walk with Darcy in the garden making Darcy feel embarrassed. Elizabeth hurries back to Jane who is better now and she expects to return home in a few days.

Caroline Bingley is more attracted by the prospect of marrying Darcy and becomes jealous of Elizabeth who receives more notice of Darcy. Miss Bingley appears more detestable by her crude effort to capture Darcy. Darcy and Elizabeth learn more about each other. Elizabeth's emotion and Darcy's logic are finely contrasted in their conversation about Bingley. Darcy, however, seems to be bewitched by Elizabeth's coolness and reticence. But Elizabeth is perhaps unaware of his feelings. Her prejudice still continues to work on her.

(*Chapter 10*)

That evening after dinner Jane comes downstairs for the first time and is received with great pleasure by everybody. Mr Bingley sits together with Jane and talks throughout the evening. Darcy takes up a book and Miss Bingley, to impress him, attempts to read a book, without success. Miss Bingley advises her brother not to have a ball at Netherfield, and then to catch the attention of Darcy paces the room and finally, in desperation, asks Elizabeth to walk with her. Darcy notices the ladies but declines the invitation to walk with them. Miss Bingley seems to be offended. Elizabeth suggests that Miss Bingley should laugh at Darcy. Then there is an exchange of ideas between Darcy and Elizabeth regarding the importance of laughter and jokes in life. Elizabeth says that others' follies make her laugh and refers to Darcy's vanity and pride. Darcy admits that he has a hardness of temper. Miss Bingley, finding herself completely overlooked, comes forward with some music, and Darcy, fearing that he is too attentive to Elizabeth, turns to it.

We get a fine example of the accurate observation and gentle irony of Jane Austen in this chapter. We also find the romance of Jane and Bingley developing well. The conversation between Darcy and Elizabeth shows both the characters revealing their pride and prejudice. Elizabeth ridicules what is wise and good by mocking Darcy and is thus guilty of poor judgment based on prejudice. Darcy seems to be confident that his own pride is controlled, and so is Elizabeth, while both are wrong. The irony in their conversation is quite evident.

(*Chapter 11*)

Jane is recovered from her illness. So, Elizabeth writes to her mother to send the carriage for their return home. Mrs Bennet wants them to remain there as long as possible so that Jane's matrimonial prospect with Mr Bingley becomes brighter. But the girls decide to leave Netherfield the next day, although Miss Bingley, out of courtesy, asks them to stay longer. Mr Bingley is really sad that Jane should depart so soon. Darcy, who feels that Elizabeth's appeal has grown very strong, wants to be rid of her presence and pointedly ignores her for the whole of the last day. When the girls arrive home, Mrs Bennet feels disappointed as she has not expected them back home so soon, while Mr Bennet is happy to welcome his two sensible daughters back.

This chapter ends the episode of the stay of Jane and Elizabeth at Netherfield and with it one small cycle of the movement of the plot, which is the first stage in the growth of love in the two pairs of lovers. Darcy's pride and his misunderstanding of Elizabeth's character, in spite of his supposed love for her, are clearly shown in this chapter. Darcy here appears as no romantic or passionate lover. He is rational and a man of calm deliberation. He deliberately detaches himself from Elizabeth in order to think deeply of the nature of his attachment to her. Mrs Bennet once again exposes her foolishness in this chapter. Miss Bingley is glad for the departure of Elizabeth but shows her courteous veneer by asking her to stay with them for a few more days.

(*Chapter 12*)

Next morning at breakfast Mr Bennet announces the visit of a stranger, a cousin, Mr Collins who, as Mr Bennet's nearest male relation, is heir to his property by entail. Mr Collins, the Rector of Hunsford Parsonage under the patronage of Lady Catherine de Bourgh, expressed his willingness, a month ago, in a pompous letter, to visit the Bennets. Mrs Bennet is not at all pleased at the prospect of entertaining a guest who will deprive her daughters of their father's property. But after listening to Collins's letter she is softened by hopes of a possible husband for one of her daughters. Mr Bennet and Elizabeth guess from the tone of the letter that Mr Collins is somewhat ridiculous and when he actually arrives he proves himself to be just that, a mixture of conceit, servility and exaggerated compliments. He incurs the displeasure of Mrs Bennet at the dinner table by asking which of the cousins has cooked the food, as Mrs Bennet informs him that they have the services of a good cook. Collins profusely apologizes for his mistake.

The arrival of the obnoxious Mr Collins begins a new episode in the novel. For, Collins's courtship of Elizabeth and Charlotte Lucas is one of the important events of the chapters that follow. In this chapter we first hear of Lady Catherine de Bourgh. Jane Austen believes that a man reveals himself by his speech and writing. Thus, she has finely revealed the character of Mr Collins by his pompous letter. Collins's compliments to the Bennet girls also give us a glimpse of his real purpose of visiting the Bennets.

(*Chapter 13*)

After dinner Mr Bennet talks with Mr Collins about his patroness Lady Catherine de Bourgh. Mr Collins becomes eloquent in her praise. Then Mr Bennet takes him to the drawing room for tea, where being invited to read to the ladies, he reads out from Fordyce's sermons boring the young ladies. As Lydia interrupts him and talks to her mother on some insignificant topic, Collins feels insulted, stops reading and offers to play backgammon with Mr Bennet.

This chapter establishes the character of Collins who is both ridiculous and conceited. He refers continually to Lady Catherine to improve his own standing. He is also hypocritical and pretentious. In this chapter we also gain an indirect view of Lady Catherine who appears to be an unpleasant personality. Mr Bennet's humorous nature and Lydia's silliness are once again displayed.

(*Chapter 14*)

Collins's poor upbringing has not made him a sensible man in spite of his training at college. On the other hand, his unexpected prosperity makes him conceited while his veneration for his patroness turns him into a servile creature. Under the advice of his patroness he has come to marry one of the Bennet girls. He starts with Jane, but on learning that she is going to be engaged, he turns to Elizabeth, being the second in line. He accompanies the Bennet girls to their aunt's house at Meryton being advised by Mr Bennet who thus wants to get rid of him. On the way they meet an army officer Mr Denny and his friend Mr Wickham, an attractive young man, who is also a commissioned officer in the army. Meanwhile Darcy and Bingley ride down the street and stop to talk to the girls. But, as soon as Darcy sees Wickham, both feel uneasy and both Darcy and Bingley leave the place soon. Mr Denny and Wickham accompany the girls to their aunt's house. They are all received cordially by the aunt, Mrs Philips, who arranges for an evening party the following day, to which she invites both Collins and Wickham.

In this chapter Collins's character is further developed. His practical attitude to marriage is demonstrated by his instant change of direction from Jane to Elizabeth as an object of marriage. Wickham, an important character in the novel, is first introduced in this chapter and his strained relation with Darcy is at once hinted at. The meeting of Elizabeth with Wickham will subsequently help to remove Elizabeth's prejudice against Darcy.

(*Chapter 15*)

The next evening when the Bennet sisters accompanied by Collins reach Meryton at the Philipses' party, they learn that Mr Wickham has already arrived. Mr Wickham appears to be the most pleasant personality and an interesting talker. So, while Collins is engaged in talking with Mrs Philips about furniture and other trifles, Elizabeth seeks opportunity to talk to Mr Wickham, particularly with a view to knowing his relation with Darcy. Soon Elizabeth gets the opportunity. Wickham tells her how Darcy's father, who loved him, intended a church living for him, but after his death Darcy deprived him of that being jealous of the latter's superior personal attraction. Wickham also informs Elizabeth that Miss Darcy also is very proud and that Darcy will marry the daughter of Lady Catherine who is dictatorial and insolent. He also hints at Darcy's hypocritical nature saying that Darcy is a past master in making friends. Elizabeth believes all this and her prejudice against Darcy is not only confirmed but increased, although she thinks that Darcy is not so bad as this.

Wickham, in this chapter, succeeds in alienating further, Darcy and Elizabeth. He serves to complicate the plot. He has enormous self-confidence to lie so blatantly, and he does so to hurt Darcy whom he hates and also to impress Elizabeth. Elizabeth is so carried away by her romantic relationship with Wickham that all her sense is lost. She is completely deceived by Wickham's story, and this is because she is already prejudiced against Darcy. This chapter also throws some light on Darcy's character although portrayed through Wickham's biased eyes. Unwittingly Wickham hints at Darcy's virtues demonstrated by his family feelings and charitable actions. Elizabeth also is not willing to believe all that Wickham has said against Darcy.

(*Chapter 16*)

The next day Elizabeth tells Jane of Wickham's accusations of Darcy. Jane, who is too good to think ill of anybody, does not wish to believe ill of either Darcy or Wickham. The Bingleys now arrive with the invitation to the promised ball at Netherfield next Tuesday. The Bingley sisters ignore all the members of the family except Jane while inviting and leave as soon as possible. Everyone is excited about the ball and while Jane thinks of dancing with Mr Bingley, Elizabeth is elated at the thought of getting an opportunity to dance with Wickham. Elizabeth, however, is upset when Collins requests her to dance with him the first two dances. Her worry is increased when her mother hints that Collins is about to propose marriage. To avoid any unpleasantness Elizabeth remains silent about any such proposal and agrees to dance with Collins. Her sisters also eagerly wait for the ball.

The first section of this chapter shows Elizabeth's totally misplaced confidence in her own prejudiced judgment of the situation. Jane Austen here wants to emphasize the fact that appearance is sometimes deceptive. There is a slight hint that Elizabeth has developed a romantic attachment to Wickham. As a contrast to this romantic relationship there is the practical materialistic proposal of Collins supported by equally materialistic Mrs Bennet. The haughtiness of the Bingley sisters is also revealed by their unmannerly behaviour towards the Bennets.

(Chapter 17)

At the Netherfield ball Elizabeth finds Wickham absent. He has gone to London ostensibly on some urgent work, but in reality, to avoid Darcy. Elizabeth becomes angry with Darcy thinking him to be the cause of Wickham's absence. She dances with Collins, rather with mortification, but she is surprised when Darcy asks her to dance with him. In the beginning they talk little but soon Elizabeth tells Darcy what she has heard about him from Wickham. Darcy feels embarrassed and immediately changes the topic. Later Jane tells Elizabeth that Wickham's remarks about Darcy are quite baseless and that Darcy is really an honourable man. But Elizabeth is so confirmed in her prejudice against Darcy that she gives no importance to Jane's words. Elizabeth and Darcy next discuss books and people's characters and Darcy warns Elizabeth about judging people falsely and too critically. Miss Bingley also warns Elizabeth that her attraction to Wickham is misplaced and that Wickham is not a trustworthy person. Elizabeth ignores her being convinced that Caroline is prejudiced. Mr Collins, despite Elizabeth's warning, goes to introduce himself to Darcy and is snubbed. Mrs Bennet's boasts to Lady Lucas of the forthcoming marriage of Jane to Bingley and Elizabeth to Collins, become embarrassing to Elizabeth, and more so for the foolish behaviour of the members of her family. The Bennets depart late in the night after exacting a promise from Mr Bingley to dine with them soon.

The chapter shows us Darcy's very real pride and prejudice in his attitude to the Bennets and Collins. Elizabeth also shows her prejudice in rejecting the information Caroline and Jane give about Wickham and Darcy. Jane's romantic relationship with Bingley is having its own course but Jane Austen is more interested in depicting the subterranean love growing in the hearts of Darcy and Elizabeth. The embarrassment of Elizabeth by her family's behaviour paves the way for her acceptance of Darcy's criticism in his letter. Mr Collins's lack of social judgment and Mrs Bennet's total ignorance of such matters are brought out in this chapter. Darcy suddenly becomes aware that his friend Bingley's marriage with Jane is nothing but a plot by the social-climbers and he thinks of thwarting this plot. Darcy's silence and his remoteness from Elizabeth clearly reveal a rift. And Bingley's plan to go to London makes us anticipate a cooling of his affair with Jane.

(*Chapter 18*)

The next morning, having got the permission to remain with Elizabeth for some time, Collins proposes to Elizabeth giving her the practical reasons for his proposal and the advantages Elizabeth will enjoy as his wife. Collins assures Elizabeth that after marrying her their entailed property will remain with the family. On Elizabeth's refusal Collins thinks it as a maiden's coyness. But Elizabeth's insistent refusal makes Collins perturbed and he says that she will never have any such offer in her life if she declines his, and expresses his hope that she will ultimately yield under her parents' wishes. Elizabeth leaves the place without any reply and decides to ask her father to handle the situation.

We learn much of Collins's character in this chapter. Collins is a comic figure. He sees Elizabeth as the right woman for all the wrong reasons. He offers marriage as a financially and socially sound contract. He thinks his offer attractive as it promises a comfortable life not only for Elizabeth but also for her family. Hence Elizabeth's rejection of this offer is an act of courage and firmness for the principle she believes in. Elizabeth is courteous and honest despite her bitter feelings against Collins. That marriage is the union of two souls and not a mere assurance of financial security is the view of Jane Austen, suggested by Elizabeth's declining the proposal of Collins.

(*Chapter 19*)

When Mrs Bennet learns from Collins about Elizabeth's refusal, she describes her daughter as headstrong and foolish and this makes Collins think it inadvisable to marry Elizabeth, as Lady Catherine has asked him to marry a sensible woman. Mrs Bennet now asks her husband to order Elizabeth to accept Collins, but with typical good sense Mr Bennet tells Elizabeth not to do so, much to the displeasure of Mrs Bennet. Mrs Bennet pleads and threatens, but Elizabeth stands firm in her decision. Finally Collins withdraws his proposal with apologies and much resentment. Now, Charlotte Lucas arrives and learns from Mrs Bennet all that has happened.

In this chapter Collins's proposal to Elizabeth comes to an end as Mr Bennet supports Elizabeth's refusal. This leaves the way clear for Charlotte Lucas's relationship with Collins to develop. Charlotte Lucas has also been brought to this scene at the right moment. As Collins has withdrawn his proposal, he is open for an alliance with any other woman. Mrs Bennet's selfish and emotional outburst in front of Elizabeth reveals her concern about the financial side of marriage. Elizabeth's calm and confident handling of the emotional pressure and remaining victorious is to be noticed.

(*Chapter 20*)

After Elizabeth's refusal of Collins's proposal the atmosphere in the Bennet family is heavy with gloom. Collins, however, sticks to his old programme and does not leave Longbourn early. To escape from the morose atmosphere of the house the Bennet sisters decide to go to Meryton. At Meryton Elizabeth enjoys meeting Wickham, discusses the ball at Netherfield and when he walks back to Longbourn with the Bennet girls, Elizabeth introduces him to her parents. A letter arrives for Jane from Miss Bingley, which informs her that Mr Bingley, who has gone to London, is not likely to return and that he is likely to marry Darcy's sister, Georgiana. Elizabeth assures Jane that it is merely a part of Miss Bingley's scheme to marry Darcy, and that Bingley will not be influenced by her to part from Jane, and he will surely return to Jane during winter. The ever gentle Jane refuses to think that her friend, Miss Bingley, is playing such a dirty game. The two sisters, however, agree not to worry their mother with this news.

In this chapter Jane Austen subtly mentions Collins's interest in Charlotte, paving the way for their engagement. Another important event is the introduction of Wickham to the Bennets by Elizabeth, thus furthering the romantic relationship between Elizabeth and Wickham. These two relationships, one practical, the other romantic, now run parallel. The letter of Miss Bingley helps to complicate the plot further by apparently making an end of Bingley's first courtship of Jane. Besides showing Collins's pretentious nature, this chapter also offers a further contrast between Elizabeth and Jane. Jane is soft, trusting and gentle. She is easily disturbed by emotions. Elizabeth is intelligent and perceptive. Yet her perception of Mr Bingley and his sister is not quite correct.

(*Chapter 21*)

The next day Charlotte remains busy attracting the attention of Collins towards her, with the ulterior motive to win him for herself. For, she is already twenty-seven and needs a husband at the earliest. Early next morning Collins pays a secret visit to Charlotte, proposes to her and is accepted with the consent of her parents. Charlotte asks Collins not to disclose the news to the Bennet sisters. So, Collins expressing his desire to visit the Bennets once more, takes his leave. Charlotte breaks the news to her friend, Elizabeth, who is shocked that her friend has consented to be the wife of such a fool. Charlotte is sure she will be happy and Elizabeth, for politeness's sake, agrees with her.

In this chapter Jane Austen presents the picture of a society which looks upon marriage of any kind as its ultimate goal. An unmarried girl in such a society has a wretched existence. Either she has to work as a poorly paid governess to wealthy children or to work as a companion to a richer person or even a rich relative, for her living. Such a girl often has to become a burden on her brother. Against this background we can understand Charlotte's efforts to get Collins as her husband. Charlotte is thus practical and clear-sighted and not romantic and idealistic like her friend, Elizabeth, in matters of marriage. The Lucas family feels happy to have a guarantee for Charlotte's economic security even at the cost of sacrificing her to a fool.

(*Chapter 22*)

Sir William Lucas arrives at Longbourn with news of the engagement between Charlotte and Collins and is met with total disbelief by Mrs Bennet and her younger daughters. Mrs Bennet is more upset than ever to think that her best friend's daughter Charlotte has not only gained a husband but will inherit Longbourn as the wife of Collins. She goes on scolding Elizabeth for a whole week and does not speak well to Mr and Mrs Lucas for a month. Mr Bennet, however, is pleased to discover that Charlotte is as foolish as his wife and more foolish than Elizabeth. To add to the distress of Mrs Bennet there is no information about the whereabouts of Mr Bingley, and Elizabeth, too, begins to doubt Bingley's faith. Collins informs in a letter to Mr Bennet about his engagement to Charlotte, which, he writes, is approved by Lady Catherine. He expresses his desire to come to Longbourn on Monday to finalize the matter with Charlotte. His arrival only further adds to the distress of Mrs Bennet who ruefully thinks of losing Longbourn to Collins.

Although this chapter does not include much action, it carries the narrative forward by indicating the passage of time and also through the analysis of the different characters. The rivalry between the two families of the Bennets and the Lucases is clearly brought out in this chapter. It is interesting to note that the first volume of the novel, as originally published, comes to a conclusion in this chapter. We have, by this time, a fairly clear idea of all the major male and female characters of the novel. The story seems to have reached a very gloomy situation here. Charlotte's marriage to Collins is a proof of the irresistible power of the economic forces controlling human lives. Bingley is taken away from Jane, and Elizabeth blames Miss Bingley and Darcy for this estrangement, thus, strengthening her prejudice against Darcy. Besides, Mrs Bennet's imprudent behaviour contributes much to the disturbing situation.

(*Chapter 23*)

A letter from Miss Bingley gives the news that they will spend the winter in London and that Mr Bingley has become more intimate with Miss Darcy. At first Elizabeth, unable to believe in Mr Bingley's attachment to Miss Darcy, thinks it to be a dirty scheme of Miss Bingley. But later, thinking of Charlotte's behaviour in accepting as her husband a fool like Collins, she develops misgivings about Bingley's nature. Jane, however, does not find anything wrong with Charlotte or Mr Bingley. She does not blame Bingley but resigns herself to fate. Yet she believes that if Mr Bingley really loves her no influence can part them. Mrs Bennet is distressed at Bingley's departure, but she hopes that he will surely return the visit in the next summer. Mr Bennet finds the matter amusing and suggests that all women benefit from being jilted and says in a mood of jest that Elizabeth should be the next to be jilted by Wickham. Meanwhile the story of ill-treatment of Wickham at the hands of Darcy is spread everywhere and Darcy is hated by everybody.

Miss Bingley's letter complicates the plot by falsely representing Bingley's love for Miss Darcy and this results in Elizabeth's intensification of prejudice against Darcy resulting in her drawing close to Wickham. We also notice the difference in the characters of Jane and Elizabeth and their views on relationships. Jane is more practical and conventional, accepting that strong emotion is no guarantee of love. Elizabeth, on the other hand, is against financially based marriages, believes in the strength of emotions and, perhaps, can more easily accept rejection. Mr Bennet's cynical remarks about rejection by lovers seem to have some truth in them.

(*Chapter 24*)

After courting Charlotte a week and finally settling the date of marriage Collins returns to his parish on Saturday and the following Monday Mrs Bennet's brother, Mr Gardiner, arrives at Longbourn with his family. Mrs Bennet tells Mrs Gardiner the whole episode relating to Bingley, Elizabeth and Collins. Mrs Gardiner, who is an intelligent, amiable and elegant woman, later tells Elizabeth that all that has happened to Jane regarding Bingley is quite natural as young men fall in and out of love easily. She suggests a visit to London to soothe Jane's feelings. Elizabeth feels hopeful to think that Jane might meet Bingley there despite Darcy's obstruction, and renew her love. During the Gardiners' stay at Longbourn Wickham is an occasional visitor. Mrs Gardiner watches Elizabeth closely and is worried by her obvious attachment to Wickham and warns Elizabeth not to be too intimate with him. Later, however, Elizabeth becomes a bit close to Wickham and, as she has little knowledge about Darcy, she seems to believe what Wickham says about Darcy's pride and ingratitude.

The Gardiners are introduced in this chapter. Mrs Gardiner has a real concern for the Bennet girls. She is intelligent and grasps the situation quickly and the practical comments she makes about the affairs of Jane and Elizabeth are quite worthwhile. Her suggestion to take Jane to London makes the plot move, as in the last chapter the situation is almost stagnant, Bingley being separated from Jane and Collins having finally chosen his wife. That violent emotions in relationships are something to be examined rationally and not to be taken on face value, as held by Mrs Gardiner, is also Jane Austen's view about romantic love.

(*Chapter 25*)

Mrs Gardiner tactfully advises Elizabeth not to encourage Wickham, for, as neither has any fortune, the relationship will be impossible. At first Elizabeth argues in favour of Wickham as the most agreeable man she has ever seen, but finally she assures Mrs Gardiner that she will try to avoid Mr Wickham. Charlotte and Collins marry and return to Hunsford. Charlotte, happy with everything, is eager to renew the friendship with Elizabeth who, despite her misgivings, agrees to visit them in March along with Charlotte's father and younger sister. Jane goes to London with the Gardiners. Hearing nothing from Caroline, she visits her and receives a polite but cold welcome. Miss Bingley's return visit to Jane is equally as brief and resentful. Jane realizes that her relationship with Bingley is at an end, particularly, as Caroline has hinted that Mr Bingley knows that Jane is in London and yet he has not come to see her. All this Jane informs Elizabeth through her letters. Meanwhile Mrs Gardiner reminds Elizabeth of her warning about Wickham who has since turned his attention to one Miss King, a rich heiress. Elizabeth knows all this and writes to Mrs Gardiner that she feels the least pain at this news.

In this chapter we notice change in three relationships. Charlotte and Collins now make a happy pair by marriage, Jane gives up all hopes of Bingley and Wickham rejects Elizabeth for a rich heiress. The theme of marriage for money is highlighted by Mrs Gardiner's advice and Wickham's courtship of an heiress. Caroline here separates Bingley and Jane further by not informing her brother about the presence of Jane in London and telling a blatant lie to Jane that her brother is not willing to meet Jane, although he knows that Jane is there. We also notice Mrs Gardiner's tactful good sense, Jane's tacit acceptance of her fate and Elizabeth's hasty and prejudicial judgment of Bingley.

(*Chapter 26*)

In March Elizabeth goes to Hunsford to visit Charlotte with Sir William and Maria Lucas. Elizabeth now looks forward to this visit with some pleasure as it will give her an opportunity to see her sister in London on the way. Her only regret is that she must leave her father. Wickham and she part as friends. The party stops in London. Elizabeth is pleased to find Jane in a happy mood, but Mrs Gardiner says that Jane is often depressed. Mrs Gardiner again warns Elizabeth against Wickham referring to his mercenary attachment to Miss King, although Elizabeth tries to defend Wickham. Now, to Elizabeth's great delight Mrs Gardiner invites her on a tour of the Lakes that summer.

This chapter marks the end of Elizabeth's first period at Longbourn. She starts visiting Hunsford. It is also the end of her innocent, uncritical opinion of Wickham, although affection for him bids her defend Wickham against the charge brought by Mrs Gardiner. The importance of money in marriage is here again emphasized. Wickham is without fortune. So, it is quite natural for him to abandon Elizabeth and turn to the rich heiress, Miss King. Elizabeth seems to understand this necessity and so she is quite resigned to her lot. Her visit to Hunsford leads to some significant development of the plot. Jane Austen has portrayed Elizabeth's state of mind in this chapter with her penetrating insight and subtle artistry. Elizabeth is now without any emotional support behind her. She is jilted by Wickham. Her relationship with Darcy is not happy. Charlotte, her dear friend, has betrayed all the values they once agreed on, by marrying Collins. The parents of Elizabeth show no sympathy in her sorrow. Elizabeth is also sad for Jane because of her separation from Bingley. And now she is going to the house of Collins where she may meet Lady Catherine, both of whom she hates.

(*Chapter 27*)

Elizabeth and the Lucases arrive at Hunsford and are received warmly by Charlotte and Collins waiting for the party. Collins thinks that by seeing the grand house with its magnificent furniture Elizabeth will repent for not marrying him, but Elizabeth who is least interested in all this, feels pity for her friend who has chosen such a foolish man for her husband. Elizabeth is, however, impressed by the neatness of the arrangements inside, made by Charlotte. At dinner Collins suggests that his guests will have the honour of getting an invitation to dine at Rosings with Lady Catherine. About the middle of the next day Lady Catherine's daughter comes with

Mrs Jenkinson with such an invitation. Elizabeth slyly remarks that the sickly and cross Miss de Bourgh will be the perfect wife for Darcy.

Here Jane Austen seems to show us the result of a marriage founded on convenience. Charlotte seems to be happy by wisely remaining deaf to the foolishness of her husband. Elizabeth's coming to Hunsford and the invitation to Rosings are indeed significant in the progress of the main plot. Jane Austen thus prepares us for Elizabeth's meeting with Lady Catherine and later with Darcy.

(*Chapter 28*)

Despite too much fuss by Collins, Elizabeth remains quiet and confident during her visit to the Rosings. The house and grounds of Lady Catherine are impressive, the Lady herself is formidable and her daughter appears insignificant. As the party enters the room Lady Catherine rises to receive them. Sir Lucas and his daughter Maria are overwhelmed with awe at the opulence. Every dish at dinner is praised lavishly by Collins and Sir William Lucas. After dinner the ladies are taken to the drawing-room where they listen to the opinions, queries and advice of Lady Catherine. Lady Catherine questions Elizabeth impertinently about her accomplishments, education and age, and Elizabeth answers to all the questions with confidence. The evening ends after various games are played and Collins drives the party home with all praise for his patroness.

We meet in this chapter Lady Catherine, the patroness of Collins, a comic character and an example of one whose false pride delights in using its power to manipulate others. She is offensive, loud, foolish and tyrannical. Collins's sycophancy towards this lady makes him also a comic character. The power and influence riches have in Austen's society is revealed by the behaviour of the Lucases. Elizabeth's personality as presented at Rosings elevates her from her circle to be looked upon with respect later by Darcy.

(*Chapter 29*)

After a week Sir William returns to Meryton satisfied that his daughter is most comfortably settled. Elizabeth stays on at

Hunsford taking long walks, chatting with Charlotte and visiting Rosings. A fortnight later, just before Easter, Collins brings the information of the arrival of Darcy at Rosings and soon Darcy comes to Hunsford with his cousin Colonel Fitzwilliam, a handsome young man of about thirty. Fitzwilliam is quite agreeable in manners while Darcy is still reserved but courteous enough to inquire of Elizabeth after the health of her family. Elizabeth provokes Darcy by asking whether he has seen Jane while in London, to which Darcy answers in the negative with some confusion giving out that he may have some role in keeping Bingley away from Jane.

In this chapter Elizabeth is once again brought into contact with Darcy. This meeting of the two protagonists shows Jane Austen's use of coincidence in her novel. Colonel Fitzwilliam is introduced here as another admirer for Elizabeth. We also notice that in his behaviour with Elizabeth, Darcy is no longer haughty and rude as he has been before. In this way Jane Austen gradually brings these two close together.

(*Chapter 30*)

On Easter Day Mr Collins and party are invited to Rosings by Lady Catherine. As Lady Catherine's attention is directed to Darcy, Mr Fitzwilliam attends to the guests and he particularly busies himself with Elizabeth whom he admires. After coffee Elizabeth plays some tune at the request of Fitzwilliam and Darcy watches both curiously. Now there is an exchange of witty, humorous and clever banter between Elizabeth and Darcy. Elizabeth accuses Darcy of being aloof and anti-social. Darcy claims that he is uncomfortable in unfamiliar company. Elizabeth replies that he merely lacks, as she does, on the piano. Darcy, however, compliments Elizabeth as a truly accomplished woman. Lady Catherine intervenes in the conversation and remarks that though Elizabeth has sung fairly well, yet she is no match to her own daughter, Anne. She goes on offering her remarks about Elizabeth's performance, which Elizabeth bears patiently and the visit ends.

In this chapter Darcy comes closer to Elizabeth revealing how much he admires her. Colonel Fitzwilliam's interest in Elizabeth also brings to the forefront her qualities and virtues.

Lady Catherine embarrasses everybody by her self-important and foolish talks. The exchange of wit between Darcy and Elizabeth shows Jane Austen's skill in employing witty dialogues and may remind one of Shakespeare's romantic heroines.

(*Chapter 31*)

Next morning Darcy visits Hunsford and finds Elizabeth alone. Elizabeth, to engage Darcy in conversation, directly asks him the reason of his and Bingley's hasty departure from Netherfield. As Darcy says that Bingley is probably not returning to Netherfield, the subject of the conversation ends there. The talk now turns to the Collinses, the success of their marriage, the distance of family homes to marital ones. Darcy now wants to test the reaction of Elizabeth to the thought of removing from Longbourn. Elizabeth expresses surprise at this statement and Darcy expresses regret and leaves a few minutes later as Charlotte and Maria return from their walk. After Darcy leaves, Charlotte remarks that he is in love with Elizabeth, to which Elizabeth does not give any importance. After this episode Darcy and Fitzwilliam visit Hunsford almost every day. Finding Darcy rather cold and reserved Charlotte thinks that Fitzwilliam is in love with Elizabeth and she hopes that they may marry.

This chapter sets the scene for Darcy's proposal to Elizabeth. Darcy is in love with Elizabeth and is ready to take her to Pemberley with him thinking that she is too good for Longbourn. In this chapter Elizabeth makes a public statement of her approval of the practical marriage of Charlotte and Collins. Charlotte here appears to be clear-sighted enough to guess about the romantic situation developing between Darcy and Elizabeth.

(*Chapter 32*)

Darcy often meets Elizabeth in the Park during her walk, which she dislikes. One day instead of Darcy, Fitzwilliam comes and has a long talk with Elizabeth during which he informs her of their departure next Saturday. He also tells Elizabeth that he shares Darcy in the guardianship of Miss Darcy. To this Elizabeth remarks sarcastically that really it is a difficult task for one to manage a girl of the true Darcy type, alone. Now, Fitzwilliam tells Elizabeth that Darcy has saved a friend from an imprudent marriage, as he does not consider that lady to be fit to become his friend's wife. Elizabeth guesses that he is talking about Bingley, although Fitzwilliam has not mentioned his name. She realizes now that it is Darcy who has separated Bingley from Jane and so she becomes more averse to Darcy. She thinks that it is Darcy's pride and his wish that Bingley marry his sister, Georgiana, that have caused sufferings to her sister. The distress caused by the thought is so intense that she suffers from severe headache and she does not go to Rosings in the evening, although invited to tea.

This chapter is another turning point in the novel. Elizabeth finds another reason to condemn Darcy to fuel her prejudice. She believes that Darcy is totally motivated by pride, and so, becoming biased, she does not reason through the possible alternatives or rational arguments in Darcy's favour. Colonel Fitzwilliam's function here is to remind Elizabeth of the importance of fortune in marriage and to inform her of Darcy's role in separating Bingley from Jane. This may be considered a coincidence in the Hardyan sense, as when Darcy is about to move close to Elizabeth, Fitzwilliam unwittingly drives him away from her.

(*Chapter 33*)

Elizabeth has been reading the letters of Jane written to her since her arrival at Kent. The letters betray her sister's lack of cheerfulness. Elizabeth is, however, comforted by the thought that Darcy, who is the cause of Jane's suffering, is not going to trouble her any more by his visit, as he is leaving Rosings soon. But to her utter dismay Darcy enters the room and to her utter surprise suddenly confesses his love for her and proposes to her saying that despite her lower social status he is unable to overcome his emotions. Assuming that Elizabeth will accept his proposal, he lets her know how much he is lowering himself by desiring to marry her. Being insulted Elizabeth retorts that she cannot return his feelings or feel grateful. She summarily rejects his proposal and says that she can never love a man as he, giving her reasons as his haughtiness in proposing to her, his interference in Jane's love affair and his ill-treatment of Wickham. Darcy makes no attempt to answer her accusations and retreats quickly. After Darcy's departure Elizabeth feels great agony and weeps for a while and composes herself when she hears the sound of Lady Catherine's carriage.

This chapter shows the negative aspects of relationships. Darcy's infatuation is not genuine and Elizabeth rightly rejects his proposal of marriage. At the same time Elizabeth's preference for romantic love is equally wrong. Both are misguided in their view of the social and financial considerations of marriage. Yet both in their talks to each other show that they can form the basis of a good relationship. They communicate, they listen and then act on what they hear. Darcy's proposal is a turning point in the career of both. Elizabeth's accusation that Darcy is ungentlemanly stops him emotionally in his tracks. But he honestly tries to overcome his pride and to love Elizabeth truly. Elizabeth, too, seems to realize that Darcy really loves her. Here starts a long process whereby she will learn to return that love later.

(*Chapter 34*)

Next morning while walking in the Park Elizabeth meets Darcy who hands her a letter, requesting her to read it, and departs. In the letter Darcy defends his conduct against the two charges brought against him by Elizabeth. He accepts the first charge of being instrumental in separating Bingley from Jane and says that he has done it as he felt that Jane's feelings for Bingley were shallow and that the family of the Bennets was of a lower rank with lack of propriety. Regarding Wickham, Darcy refers to his weak and dissolute nature. Darcy's father, who loved Wickham, recommended him, at his death, to the best living falling vacant in the Pemberley estate. But as Wickham preferred to enter the law rather than the church, Darcy gave him three thousand pounds and Wickham soon squandered that amount and later applied for the vacant living in the Pemberley estate. As Darcy refused to grant him the post, he revenged himself by planning an elopement with Georgiana, which was, however, prevented at the last moment. Since then

Wickham maligned the character of Darcy everywhere. Finally, Darcy suggests that Elizabeth can verify all this with Colonel Fitzwilliam.

The letter of Darcy is a turning point in the novel. The use of letters to clear up mysteries or provide explanations is quite common in the fiction of the time. In this chapter Darcy's letter is intended to draw Darcy and Elizabeth together. The letter throw much light on Darcy's character. Darcy's decision about Bingley's relationship with Jane is proud and overbearing, based on an incorrect view of Jane and a prejudiced view of her family. But what he has done, is with a sincere desire to protect his friend from making an inferior alliance. His treatment of Wickham is quite justified. Darcy's letter shows his wisdom and generous spirit. Darcy is not only enlightened but he is also forthright. He shows in his letter how Elizabeth has considered the situation from a limited vantage point. And, perhaps, after this Elizabeth begins to realize that her prejudice against Darcy is not based on strong grounds.

(*Chapter 35*)

Elizabeth reads Darcy's letter with a strong prejudice, unwilling to believe his account of the Bingley and Jane episode, and as for Wickham's story she very much wishes it to be false. But she is very much stirred by the letter and reads it again and again. She remembers that Darcy's story of the planned elopement is supported by Colonel Fitzwilliam's reaction to her comment about Georgiana. Besides Wickham's attention to Mary King after being close to Elizabeth shows his unscrupulous and mercenary nature. Darcy may be proud, but he never has acted wrongly. Because of the reserved nature of Jane, Darcy has thought of her feeling for Bingley superficial and the behaviour of her mother and the younger sisters at Netherfield also have been unbecoming. Elizabeth now seems to realize that she has been blinded by prejudice and her judgments about Darcy and Wickham have been totally wrong. She feels greatly disturbed in mind and returns to the Parsonage from her walk to be informed that Colonel Fitzwilliam has been waiting for about an hour to whom Darcy has joined a few minutes ago, to take leave of her.

This chapter shows a detailed analysis of the factors that help Elizabeth change her mind. Such an analysis of character is rarely to be found in the fiction of the time. Elizabeth understands that her ability to judge human character of which she has been proud, is not sound. This is the heart of the chapter and, in many ways, the heart of the novel. The first sign of her increasing maturity is found when on re-reading the account of Jane and Bingley's relationship, she realizes the truth of Darcy's comments. Jane indeed seems indifferent to Bingley, and the behaviour of her family clearly shows its inferiority. Wickham's hypocrisy and meanness also become clear to Elizabeth when she coolly and rationally considers what Darcy has mentioned about him in his letter. This chapter marks the key change in Elizabeth. From now on she tries to see things clearly. She now knows the true natures of both Wickham and Darcy, the real reason for Bingley's departure, the truth about her family and her own faults of pride and prejudice. She now bids adieu to her romantic love for Wickham or Fitzwilliam and turns her attention to the reality of Darcy.

(*Chapter 36*)

The next morning Darcy and Fitzwilliam left Rosings and the Hunsford party is again invited to dinner by Lady Catherine. Seeing Elizabeth in low spirits Lady Catherine asks her to stay longer at Hunsford, but Elizabeth sticks to her previous plan of going back home. Lady Catherine is told that Elizabeth's uncle is going to send his servant to escort Elizabeth and Maria. Elizabeth is relieved of her sad thoughts of regret and pain at the dinner at Rosings — regret on the behaviour of her mother and sisters leading Darcy to detach Bingley from Jane and pain for the fact of Jane's losing Bingley as her husband and also because of her wrong estimate of Wickham's character. After this she visits Rosings almost frequently and at parting Lady Catherine wishes her and Maria a good journey and extends invitation to them to come to Hunsford again next year.

Elizabeth feels upset by Darcy's comments about her family but realizes that those are painfully true. She passes her final week at Hunsford being depressed by the thoughts of Jane and

Wickham. Lady Catherine's behaviour towards Elizabeth seems to have a little mellowed down and Elizabeth appears to be less prejudiced about her.

(*Chapter 37*)

On Saturday morning after breakfast Elizabeth leaves Hunsford with Maria, sincerely thanking Collins for the visit although she does not join Collins in his praise of Lady Catherine. Collins speaks of Charlotte as an ideal partner and Elizabeth honestly agrees to it. The party leaves for London where they will stay with the Gardiners for a few days before returning to Longbourn with Jane. Elizabeth does not tell Jane of Darcy's proposal and his letter immediately, as she thinks it prudent to keep these secret till they reach hone.

This transitional chapter takes us from Hunsford to London. Elizabeth approves of Charlotte's marriage with Collins, though she has no regret for refusing Collins. We now eagerly wait for further developments at Longbourn.

(*Chapter 38*)

In the second week of May Elizabeth, Maria and Jane set out homewards from London. Kitty and Lydia meet them on the way to take them in the carriage sent by Mr Bennet. The girls have their dinner at an inn and Lydia goes on talking about the bonnet she has purchased, about the military officers stationed there and about Wickham's marrying Miss King not coming off. On reaching Longbourn the girls are welcomed by Mr and Mrs Bennet. A large party gathers at the dinner table where all the Lucases are present. In the afternoon Lydia proposes to walk to Meryton, which Elizabeth opposes for fear of seeing Wickham there. Soon Elizabeth finds that her parents are discussing the proposal of going to Brighton.

In this chapter for the first time we hear Lydia talk at length and see her as a real character and find her as immature, self-centred, unpractical and interested only in flirtation and marriage. The information that Wickham is not marrying Miss King is important and ominous, too. It is Lydia who gives the information and Elizabeth has reason to be worried.

(*Chapter 39*)

The next morning Elizabeth relates to Jane about Darcy's proposal and her refusal. Jane is surprised to hear this, but sympathises with Darcy at his disappointment on Elizabeth's rejection of his proposal. When Elizabeth tells her of the wickedness of Wickham, Jane finds it hard to believe. But as Wickham is leaving the neighbourhood soon, Jane advises Elizabeth not to reveal Wickham's true nature to the Longbourn society. Elizabeth, however, conceals from Jane Darcy's part in Bingley's absence, as it might hurt Jane. Observing Jane's tender feeling for Bingley existing still, Elizabeth feels sad. Mrs Bennet mentions Jane's unhappiness and thinks that Bingley has betrayed Jane. She resentfully talks about Charlotte and Collins and bitterly thinks that Collins must always be talking about their estate which he will occupy, after Mr Bennet's death, by entail.

Elizabeth is growing in this chapter. She finds that she has been wrong in taking Wickham by his appearance. She has also failed to judge Darcy's goodness. She admits her faults to Jane. Her love and consideration for Jane stops her from revealing to her Darcy's role in separating Bingley from Jane. Her decision not to reveal Wickham's true character contributes to Lydia's elopement, as Elizabeth realizes later.

(*Chapter 40*)

The regiment is leaving Meryton and all the young ladies in the neighbourhood except Jane and Elizabeth feel sad. But Kitty and Lydia are particularly dejected. Lydia's depression is soon over as she is invited by Mrs Forster, the wife of the colonel of the regiment, to accompany them to Brighton. Both Elizabeth and Jane try to dissuade Lydia from accepting the invitation. But Mr Bennet thinks that Lydia needs to go in order to learn the realities of life and her own insignificance. Meanwhile, Elizabeth meets Wickham several times. On the last day of his stay at Meryton Wickham dines with other officers at Longboum. His affair with Miss King being over, Wickham now turns to court Elizabeth again, to her utter annoyance. Elizabeth gives him the clear hint that she knows the truth about him from Darcy. Wickham is embarrassed. The two part with mutual civility. Lydia leaves for Meryton with Mrs Forster. The next morning they will leave for Brighton.

In this chapter we see more of Lydia's self-centred, flighty nature. Her visit to Brighton gives her an opportunity to elope with Wickham. Her relationship with Wickham starts with the end of his relationship with Elizabeth who now sees the difference between appearance and reality. Mr Bennet reveals himself as a soft-minded father who cannot control his children. Elizabeth rightly judges the true nature of her father. The letter of Darcy has made her more clear-sighted and responsible in her dealings with the people around her.

(*Chapter 41*)

The Bennets are not a happy couple. Mr Bennet has no respect for his wife and he delights in mocking her. Elizabeth, because of Darcy's comments on her family, is also aware of the disadvantages of her family background. As the regiment has left Meryton, life there has become very dull and boring. Elizabeth, however, is excited by the prospect of a tour to the Lake District with the Gardiners. But the plans are changed and the holiday is cut short because of Mr Gardiner's heavy engagement. Instead of the Lake Districts they will visit Derbyshire a fortnight later. Elizabeth is disappointed by the change in the programme and also for excluding Jane from the tour. Four weeks later the Gardiners come and set off the next morning with Elizabeth. After visiting many places in Derbyshire the party reaches Lambton and Mrs Gardiner suggests visiting Pemberley which is not far away. Being informed that Darcy's family is not there, Elizabeth agrees to visit Pemberley.

This chapter begins by describing the failure of a marriage made from affection and physical attraction and its bad effects on the children. Mr Bennet has made an unwise choice of a wife and now feels no affection for her. He has also given up his parental responsibilities and only watches the absurdities occurring in the household. Elizabeth's trip to Pemberley has been definitely contrived by the novelist to help her correct the errors she has made so far, concerning Darcy. Lydia's departure from the protective custody of her parents creates a threat for her. This chapter prepares the reader for the revelation of Darcy's innate goodness and Lydia's elopement with Wickham.

(*Chapter 42*)

Pemerley is very charming and pleasant. The park is quite large and colourful. Ascending for half a mile the party finds the Pemberley House, a magnificent stone building at a distance. They come down the hill, cross a bridge over a stream in front of the house and enter the house to see the inside. The housekeeper obliges them and speaks highly of her master, Darcy. The party next walks outside in the garden. Suddenly Darcy appears. Both he and Elizabeth feel embarrassed. Elizabeth introduces him to the Gardiners. Darcy also wants to introduce his sister, who is coming there the next day with Bingley, to her. Elizabeth is struck by the change in him. The Gardiners are full of praise for Darcy. Elizabeth has to admit that her original judgment of Darcy was mistaken, just as it was of Wickham. Mrs. Gardiner also wonders how such a nice and good a man like Darcy can do any harm to Wickham. Elizabeth also goes on thinking about the civility of Darcy.

At Pemberley Elizabeth has the privilege of seeing the elegance, kindness and good temper of Darcy. Darcy has already admitted in chapter 31 that he does not open his heart to strangers. It is only at Pemberley that Elizabeth sees the real Darcy, a man of taste and good sense. Elizabeth now finds that Darcy has changed and she, too, is now seeing him without prejudice. She not only sees him as someone for whom she can feel respect and gratitude, but also as someone whom she likes. Darcy also seems to have lost much of his pride. Meeting the Gardiners Darcy realizes that Elizabeth's family does include some noteworthy people. Darcy and Elizabeth now begin to converge to each other.

(*Chapter 43*)

Darcy brings his sister to see Elizabeth on the day she arrives. Elizabeth is flattered by this prompt visit. Soon Bingley comes and joins them. Elizabeth finds Miss Darcy not proud as she has heard about her, but exceedingly shy and gentle. Bingley's kind and familiar manner also removes Elizabeth's displeasure for him. Elizabeth is also happy to find that Bingley is not attracted to Miss Darcy, rather he inquires after Jane. Before leaving, Darcy invites Elizabeth and the Gardiners to dinner at Pemberley and Miss Darcy also joins him in extending the invitation. The Gardiners feel that Mr Darcy is in love with their niece. Elizabeth reconsiders her feelings and wants to please

Darcy and wonders whether to encourage a second proposal. In the evening she and her aunt decide to return the compliment to Miss Darcy by visiting Pemberley the next day.

Elizabeth's meeting with Georgiana is important. It proves Darcy's real trust in Elizabeth. The appearance of Bingley is significant in the renewal of his romantic relationship with Jane. Darcy's love for Elizabeth is judged by the Gardiners as genuine and their judgment is to be trusted. The change in Darcy's behaviour works a change in the mind of Elizabeth who begins to think of marrying Darcy a real possibility. Jane Austen tactfully brings the situations in favour of the protagonists.

(*Chapter 44*)

At Pemberley Elizabeth and Mrs Gardiner are politely received by Miss Darcy. The Bingley sisters also are present there. Miss Bingley, who has been watching Elizabeth closely, does not speak for about a quarter of an hour. Later, when Darcy enters the room she sarcastically asks Elizabeth whether the regiment's departure has not been a great loss to her family, in order to discredit Elizabeth in the eyes of Darcy. Darcy perceives the malicious suggestion in the question and restrains his indignation with some difficulty. Elizabeth and her aunt depart soon afterwards. After they leave, Miss Bingley criticizes Elizabeth's looks, manner and self-sufficiency and reminds Darcy of his poor opinion of Elizabeth. Darcy, though annoyed, tells her that he considers Elizabeth one of the handsomest women of his acquaintance. After returning to Lambton, Elizabeth and Mrs Gardiner discuss about everything and everybody they have seen at Pemberley, except Darcy.

Miss Bingley's behaviour with Elizabeth betrays her jealous and uncivilized nature. She is defeated by Elizabeth's dignified behaviour and Darcy's calm reactions to her attack against Elizabeth. Darcy and Elizabeth now seem to have discovered their love only after establishing it firmly on a foundation of experience and mutual understanding, belying the notion of love at first sight or romantic love as a proper guide for marriage. Darcy's pride and Elizabeth's prejudice are gone and Jane Austen thus paves the way for their union at the end.

(*Chapter 45*)

Elizabeth is worried for not receiving any letter from Jane since her arrival at Lambton. Soon two letters from Jane arrive. One says that Lydia has eloped to Scotland with Wickham and that Jane believes that Wickham intends to marry Lydia. The second letter reveals that Wickham does not intend to marry Lydia at all and has not gone to Gretna Green, rather he is traced in London by Colonel Forster who along with Mr Bennet has set out to find the couple. Jane asks Elizabeth to return to Longbourn immediately. As the Gardiners have gone out for a walk, Elizabeth is just about to rush out to find her uncle, when Darcy comes. Elizabeth is so concerned that she discloses the contents of the letters to Darcy. She blames herself for not revealing Wickham's true character. Darcy becomes thoughtful and silent and assures her of his help in this matter in all possible ways. Promising to convey to his sister Elizabeth's apologies for not dining at Pemberley as arranged and also promising to conceal the unhappy secret from her and others Darcy departs. Mr and Mrs Gardiner arrive soon after and are distressed to hear the news and arrangements for going to Longbourn are immediately made.

Lydia's elopement is revealed in this chapter. This elopement is a representation of sensual relationships condemned by Jane Austen through Elizabeth. We find here that Wickham is, in reality, more vicious than is ever thought of. Lydia appears to us in her deed as a socially irresponsible and a horribly innocent girl who is in real danger because of her foolishness and inexperience. The news of Lydia's elopement changes everything for Elizabeth. Her family is obviously inferior to Darcy's. And this scandal regarding Lydia will much lower their family in Darcy's estimation. Fearing, therefore, that Darcy will cease to love her, Elizabeth now realizes how much he means to her. But, in fact, Darcy does not condemn her as his family also had once been similarly threatened by Wickham. He has overcome his pride and prejudice and extends his helping hand to Elizabeth. And this is the first time Elizabeth has actually shown that she needs help. This chapter also illustrates how in Jane Austen's time family pride, family honour and family responsibilities have been powerful factors in morality. Hence, Elizabeth thinks that the impropriety committed by

Lydia will taint the lives of her sisters as well. Mr Bennet is also very much affected by this incident which he considers the consequence of his neglect and mistaken indulgence.

(*Chapter 46*)

On their way to Longbourn Elizabeth and the Gardiners speculate on whether Wickham will marry Lydia. While Mr Gardiner is hopeful of Wickham's marrying Lydia, Elizabeth is not inclined to agree with him as she knows the true nature of Wickham. She blames herself for not warning Lydia earlier about Wickham. On reaching home Elizabeth and Jane comfort each other. Elizabeth learns from Jane that their father is in London and that he will not write again unless he has any news of Lydia. Jane also shows Elizabeth Lydia's parting letter left with Mrs Forster. Mrs Bennet foolishly fears that Mr Bennet will fight a duel with Mr Wickham, get killed and leave all of them paupers. Mr Gardiner comforts her by saying that he will bring Mr Bennet back from London and then the two together will make plans to trace the eloped couple. Mrs Bennet becomes cheerful at the prospect of Lydia's marriage. The Bennet sisters engage themselves in discussing about the eloped couple and the steps their father might take to find them out.

In this chapter we find Elizabeth making a merciless analysis of her family and not sparing herself for concealing Wickham's real nature. She blames herself for not warning Lydia about Wickham before her trip to Brighton. These are indications of her growing wisdom and maturity. Mrs Bennet by her talks reveals the same silly nature as she has shown before. Mary with her dry and useless platitudes appears to be as removed from the realities of life as ever. Lydia has no idea of the effect of her action on the family or herself. Her letter to Harriet exposes her at once as an irresponsible, foolish young girl. Jane Austen has shown her insight into different types of characters by presenting them through different styles of expression they use.

(*Chapter 47*)

Mr Gardiner sets off for London the next morning as no communication from Mr Bennet arrives. At London he finds Mr Bennet who plans to inquire at all the chief hotels of

London for the fugitives. Mr Gardiner writes to Mr Forster to inform him of any friends and acquaintances of Wickham with whom he might possibly stay. Elizabeth has never heard of any relations of Wickham and thinks that his companions in the regiment might give some information. Meanwhile a letter from Collins addressed to Mr Bennet arrives and it contains only pompous condolences and a quite unchristian condemnation of Lydia, advising Mr Bennet to cast off his unworthy daughter and leave her to reap the fruit of her own offence. Collins also expresses satisfaction at having escaped from entering into relationship with such a family. Mr Gardiner's next letter informs that Wickham has incurred heavy gambling debts. Mr Bennet is persuaded to return home. Mrs Gardiner also leaves for London with her children. Mr Bennet arrives the following day as calm and philosophical as usual and makes himself responsible for all that has happened.

In this chapter there is little action. Collins's letter shows his hypocrisy and lack of Christian charity. Mr Bennet's recognition of his own fault indicates his awakening to his duties as a father, which he has so far neglected. Wickham's prodigal nature is revealed and it adds more stain to his character. Mr Gardiner's efforts to find out the runaway pair shows his genuine concern for the Bennet family. This chapter also marks the passage of time since the elopement.

(*Chapter 48*)

Two days after Mr Bennet's return he receives a letter from Mr Gardiner informing him that the eloped couple have been found and that they are going to marry soon. Wickham has agreed to marry Lydia on condition that Lydia should be promised an equal share of five thousand pounds in her mother's property and that Mr Bennet should pay him an annuity of one hundred pounds till Mr Bennet is alive. Mr Gardiner believes that after paying off his creditors Wickham will still have some money left and so he has agreed to the condition of Wickham and asks Mr Bennet to give his consent. The news is a great relief to Jane and Elizabeth. Mr Bennet, however, suspects that Wickham has been given money by Mr Gardiner to make him agree to marry Lydia. He retires to the library to write the letter of consent. Jane and Elizabeth go away to give the good news to everybody. Mrs Bennet's joy knows no bounds when she hears the news and is ready to make arrangements for the marriage. While Jane thinks Wickham has a true love for Lydia, Elizabeth is doubtful about Lydia's being happy with the husband she has found.

Here also we find a loveless marriage based on financial considerations. In fact Wickham has been bribed to marry Lydia. Jane Austen here shows how the action of a single member of the family affects everybody else in the family far and near. Mr Bennet agrees to pay Wickham's blackmail amount so that his other daughters' honour is saved. Even Mr Gardiner, an uncle with children, arranges the settlement with Wickham, lest any stigma spreads to his branch of the family. Elizabeth shows her independence and sensitivity when she questions a society that prefers a loveless marriage for the sake of reputation, to no marriage at all. Mrs Bennet's reactions to the marriage are quite wrong as she shows no real awareness of the moral problems of Wickham's real character, being interested only in the status of marriage.

(*Chapter 49*)

When the Bennets married they had at first been confident that they would bear a son to inherit their estate and so Mr Bennet had not saved anything from his annual income. By the time their five daughters had been born, it was too late to start saving. Without any savings it is now difficult for Mr Bennet to repay Mr Gardiner whatever he might have personally spent on Lydia. Still he is determined to find out the extent of Mr Gardiner's assistance and free himself from the obligations as soon as possible. Of course, there is no difficulty in agreeing to Wickham's conditions as Lydia can easily have an equal share of her mother's fortune of five thousand pounds and regarding the annuity of one hundred pounds, Mr Bennet has already been spending that amount annually on Lydia. Elizabeth meanwhile regrets that she ever told Darcy about the elopement, for, now there seems to be no need for anyone to know about the scandalous event. She knows that Darcy cannot be expected to marry into a disgraced family. But what she has learnt and seen of Darcy has convinced her that Darcy and she are in fact perfectly suited. She is now anxious to gain Darcy's esteem. News of the wedding spreads. Mr Bennet refuses Lydia money for clothes, but eventually allows the couple to visit Longbourn after the wedding when Jane and Elizabeth request him to do so. Wickham is to join a northern regiment after his marriage.

This chapter continues to show the importance of the financial side of marriage. Like Lydia's and Wickham's, the Bennets' relationship had been based on physical attraction and so it has been an unhappy and financially unstable marriage. This makes Elizabeth realize how much she values Darcy as her future husband. She now learns that the right relationship is the one that meets, answers and complements and not the one that merely flatters and agrees. Another important point to note in this chapter is that the extent of Mr Gardiner's financial help to make Wickham agree to the marriage is kept vague.

(*Chapter 50*)

Lydia and Wickham marry in London and on the very day of their marriage come to Longbourn to stay for ten days. Mrs Bennet warmly welcomes the couple, while Mr Bennet is reserved. The couple seem unembarrassed. While Lydia talks on in her flippant, irresponsible manner about her elopement, her ring and her married status, Wickham also is his usual self, talking and smiling. Lydia, while describing her wedding to Elizabeth and Jane lets slip the fact that Darcy had attended her wedding. Elizabeth is amazed and rather than question Lydia, writes to Mrs Gardiner to ascertain the details about Darcy's part in the marriage.

Lydia's irresponsible and self-centred nature is shown here in detail. Wickham is shameless and talks as if nothing untoward has happened. He does not have any love for Lydia and it is the force of Lydia's love for romance that led to the elopement and the other developments. Another important event of this chapter is Elizabeth's discovery that Darcy was at the wedding of the two people whom he must have detested. Her attempt to discover the truth will later reveal to her Darcy's true generosity.

(*Chapter 51*)

Mrs Gardiner replies to Elizabeth's letter informing her of the details of Darcy's part in Lydia's marriage. With the help of Mrs Younge, Wickham's confidante, Darcy traced the runaway couple. He first tried to persuade Lydia to go back to her parents, but as she was adamant, he with great difficulty made Wickham agree to marry Lydia by paying off all his debts and agreeing to his conditions of marriage. After doing so much Darcy had met Mr Gardiner, told him everything, got his consent and exacted a promise from him to keep his share in the affair a secret. He said to Mr Gardiner that he had done all this as he thought himself responsible for Lydia's ignorance of the true nature of Wickham. But Mrs Gardiner suggests in her letter that perhaps it is out of love for Elizabeth that Darcy has done all this. She ends her letter by hinting that it would be a good thing if Elizabeth were to marry Darcy. Elizabeth is overcome by all that Darcy has done. She begins to think very high of Darcy. Wickham interrupts as she is reading the letter. Elizabeth manages the conversation with great skill and without being unnecessarily rude lets him know that she is aware of his true nature. Wickham feels embarrassed and Elizabeth suggests that they should forget the past and live in future like brother and sister.

Elizabeth has learnt from Mrs Gardiner the extent to which Darcy has helped Lydia. Darcy has overcome his pride and prejudice to do the right thing. Elizabeth's feelings towards him are even more positive as she has now the clear approval of her aunt, Mrs Gardiner, whose advice she values, for marriage with Darcy. Yet she cannot expect to have Darcy whom she has once refused and who certainly will not like to be the brother-in-law of Wickham, by marrying her. Once again the theme of family pride and honour is reinforced. The novel, however, is fast moving towards a happy close. Elizabeth here completely frees herself from the charm of Wickham who, though exposed, does not admit his lies.

(*Chapter 52*)

Lydia and Wickham leave for Newcastle after ten days. Mrs Bennet is depressed, but her gloom is over at the news that Mr Bingley is to visit Netherfield in a few days. She requests her husband to invite Mr Bingley to Longbourn on his arrival, but Mr Bennet curtly refuses to do so. But to Mrs Bennet's great surprise Bingley comes to Longbourn with Darcy of his own accord on the third morning after his arrival. Although Jane and Elizabeth are greatly delighted to have their favourites, they sit through the visit without much visible embarrassment. But, Mrs Bennet invites them to dine at their place after a few days.

Elizabeth recognizes that Darcy's arrival at Longbourn is a signal that his affection for her has not been destroyed by Lydia's elopement with Wickham. Mrs Bennet's bitterness towards Darcy, an example of uninformed prejudice, makes Elizabeth feel more insecure about him. Darcy is now seen to reassess Jane's and Bingley's relationship and also the feelings of Elizabeth towards him. Jane Austen has skilfully brought Mr Bingley and Jane together again so that their love may develop and ultimately culminate in marriage.

(*Chapter 53*)

Darcy's silent, grave and indifferent behaviour during his visit makes Elizabeth ponder about the cause. Jane now comes and tells Elizabeth that she will treat Mr Bingley as her friend and nothing more, which Elizabeth refuses to believe. On Tuesday Darcy and Bingley come to the Bennets for the dinner. It is a big party. Bingley sits next to Jane at the table, but Darcy takes his seat by the side of Mrs Bennet, far away from Elizabeth. Even at the cards table Elizabeth is disappointed when she does not get Darcy as her partner. Mrs Bennet is, however, satisfied on seeing Bingley's behaviour with Jane although Jane refuses to admit her love for Bingley.

In this chapter the suspense increases. Elizabeth is frustrated at not being able to be close to Darcy. She now admits his right not to be humiliated by rejection and regrets having rejected him. Once again appearances deceive Elizabeth making her fear the worst. She now recognizes the basic decency and gentlemanliness of Darcy. Meanwhile Jane's and Bingley's romance develops easily and quickly, although Jane refuses to admit it.

(*Chapter 54*)

Darcy leaves for London on an urgent business. Bingley calls at Longbourn and is warmly welcomed. He begins to visit the Bennets very often. On one such visit he proposes to Jane and is accepted. Jane confides this secret to Elizabeth. Soon the whole family is in a jovial mood. Mr Bennet congratulates Jane on having been engaged to Bingley and Mrs Bennet is delighted to have yet another daughter engaged. Jane learns from Bingley that he did not know that she was in London during the spring and realizes that Miss Bingley is responsible for this. She now finds that people are not necessarily as good as she would like to think them to be.

Jane and Bingley are united in this chapter. Throughout their relationship the proposal and engagement are romantic. The young girl accepts the dashing hero as the happiest creature in the world. Their relationship is quite unrealistic. As Mr Bennet observes that it will succeed because both of them are perfectly good-tempered. The chapter is significant in that one important line of the sub-plot concerning Jane and Bingley is concluded. Elizabeth realizes that she will never have Jane's happiness as she will never be the perfect romantic heroine. She is however happy that Bingley has not betrayed his friend Darcy by telling Jane about Darcy's role in separating him from Jane. For, a knowledge of this might have made Jane prejudiced against Darcy.

(*Chapter 55*)

A week after Jane's engagement one morning Lady Catherine visits the Bennets. She is patronizing and unfriendly. She leads Elizabeth off for a walk into the copse and wants to know if she is engaged to Darcy, as she has heard. She officiously declares that she has plans for Darcy and Lady Anne, her daughter, to marry. She adds that considering the inferiority of the Bennets and the disgrace brought into the family by Lydia, a marriage with Elizabeth would be degrading for Darcy. As Elizabeth says that she is not engaged to Darcy, Lady Catherine demands an assurance from her that she will never accept any such proposal from Darcy. Elizabeth curtly refuses to give such an assurance and Lady Catherine returns to her carriage in high temper threatening Elizabeth all the way and drives away.

As Darcy and Elizabeth are coming close to each other Lady Catherine stands as an almost impregnable obstacle between the two. Lady Catherine represents the traditional view of the rigid class structure with inflexible boundaries between the classes. She fails to realize that the love between Darcy and Elizabeth is not the result of an impulsive infatuation, nor a reflection of Elizabeth's social ambitions to rise above her class by marrying Darcy, but rather the union of two sensible people. Her officious and stubborn nature presents her as an epitome of false pride and prejudice. Elizabeth's victory over Lady Catherine lies in the fact that she stands up for herself as a person, shows courage, argues rationally and boldly and loves Darcy enough to fight for him.

(*Chapter 56*)

After the departure of Lady Catherine, Elizabeth feels uneasy. She wonders how the false report about her engagement to Darcy has spread. She suspects the Lucases as the originator of the rumour. She fears that Lady Catherine might advise Darcy not to propose to her, and if Darcy fails to return to Netherfield on the appointed day it may be taken as a sign of his acceptance of his aunt's advice. A letter from Collins reaches Mr Bennet congratulating him on Jane's engagement but warning that acceptance of Darcy's proposal to Elizabeth will incur the wrath of Lady Catherine. Mr Bennet has knowledge of Elizabeth's dislike for Darcy and not of her changed attitude. So, to amuse her he conveys the news to her and she pretends to take it very lightly.

This chapter contains Elizabeth's final trial. Elizabeth now is in a suspended state of confusion. Even now she is not confident about Darcy. Yet she seems to be hurt by the fact that even her father can ridicule the idea of Darcy's ever loving her. Collins shows his peculiar notion of Christian forgiveness by advising Mr Bennet to forgive Lydia and Wickham, as a Christian, but never to admit them in his sight nor allow their names to be heard.

(*Chapter 57*)

A few days after Lady Catherine's visit Darcy returns to Netherfield and visits Longbourn with Bingley. Jane, Elizabeth and Kitty accompany the gentlemen on a walk outside. Bingley and Jane wanting to be alone walk in advance and Kitty goes to the Lucases to meet Maria. Elizabeth and Darcy are now together. Elizabeth plucks up the courage to thank Darcy for what he has done for Lydia and explains to him that she has learnt about the secret not from her uncle or aunt but from a hint carelessly thrown by Lydia. Darcy declares that he has done everything for Lydia out of his genuine interest in Elizabeth. He asks her if she feels about him as she did last April. Elizabeth now explains how much her feelings have changed and Darcy, too, tells her of his love in a way that shows how genuine it is. Now both Darcy and Elizabeth discuss their faults. Elizabeth admits how ashamed she is of her previous dealings with Darcy and how Darcy's letter has removed her former prejudices. Darcy also confesses how he took to heart Elizabeth's accusations of his ungentlemanly behaviour and makes his father responsible for developing his own haughty mien. He explains that what he has learnt about Elizabeth's reaction to Lady Catherine makes him realize how much she cares for him. He also tells Elizabeth that it is he who has advised Bingley to propose to Jane when he realizes how much the two love each other.

The story of the novel almost reaches its conclusion in this chapter. The most important events in the novel are the changes of heart Elizabeth and Darcy undergo. We see here clearly the change in Darcy and Elizabeth. Darcy now respects Elizabeth's family and thinks only of her and receives Elizabeth's unexpected acceptance with both gratitude and happiness. Elizabeth is quick to admit that she is selfish and thanks Darcy for his generosity, being fully aware how his pride must have been injured. Darcy also has learnt his lesson. Both realize their faults. Their attitudes to each other are now based on respect and affection.

(*Chapter 58*)

At night Elizabeth tells everything to Jane who takes some time to believe it and some more time to assure herself that her sister really loves Darcy. Elizabeth tells Jane that since the previous April her feelings towards Darcy have undergone a radical change. Next morning Bingley and Darcy again visit Longbourn. To allow Jane and Bingley all by themselves Mrs Bennet proposes that Darcy and Elizabeth should go to Oakham Mount. During the walk it is decided that Darcy will apply for Mr Bennet's consent in the evening while Elizabeth should seek her mother's consent to their marriage. Accordingly Darcy meets Mr Bennet and gets his approval. But Mr Bennet, doubtful of Elizabeth's love for Darcy, calls her to him and Elizabeth assures her father of her changed attitude and tells him of Darcy's goodness and nobility and discloses to him the help Darcy has rendered secretly in Lydia's affairs. Mr Bennet is happy and Mrs Bennet's joy also knows no bounds when she learns the news.

Elizabeth in this chapter reconciles her family to her marriage with Darcy, overcoming their prejudice. The theme of appearance and reality takes a new turn here. Elizabeth sees the reality of Darcy and has to make others see through the appearance. Her defence of Darcy's pride, her boldness in speaking of her attitude to Darcy to her father, show that she is genuinely in love with Darcy. To Jane Austen love is not merely a sensual attachment, it must stand the test of time. Hence, Jane and Elizabeth will have a successful and happy marriage.

(*Chapter 59*)

Elizabeth now becomes familiar with Darcy. One day she playfully asks him when he actually started loving her. As Darcy is unable to give her any information about it, Elizabeth helps him with clever guesswork. Darcy, however, comments that her spirit and kindness to Jane first attracted him to her. Elizabeth argues that he loved her as she did not seek his approval or flatter him like other women. The same day Darcy writes to Lady Catherine informing her of his engagement with Elizabeth, Elizabeth writes to Mrs Gardiner giving her the happy news and inviting her to Pemberley at Christmas, and Mr Bennet writes to Collins in reply to the latter's letter of warning, asking him in his usual caustic manner to console Lady Catherine in her disappointment. Collins, instead of replying to the letter of Mr Bennet, comes with his wife to the Lucas Lodge, to be out of the way of the wrath of Lady Catherine. Darcy bears well with Elizabeth's family, but Elizabeth now realizes the difference in quality between them.

This chapter, like the next one, completes the unfinished business in the novel. We learn the reasons for Darcy's attraction for Elizabeth from both Darcy and Elizabeth. Elizabeth now prepares herself physically and mentally for her transition to Pemberley. It is interesting to note that in Jane Austen's world there is very little display of passion. Darcy and Elizabeth seem to be contented to talk, analyse and reason over their love rather than to exchange words of passion and emotion.

(*Chapter 60*)

Darcy and Elizabeth, now married, go to Pemberley. Bingley and Jane stay at Netherfield only for a year and then Bingley purchases an estate in Derbyshire, thirty miles away from Pemberley and settles down there. Mr Bennet misses Elizabeth very much and so visits Pemberley often. Kitty improves herself by spending most of her time with her two elder sisters. Mary stays at home attending her mother. Wickham and Lydia's relationship soon declines. Their lack of love is now paralleled by a lack of money. Lydia often writes to Jane and Elizabeth for money which they send according to their limits. Miss Bingley and Lady Catherine are greatly displeased with Darcy for having married Elizabeth, but in due course they get reconciled and continue good relations with Darcy. Georgiana, now permanently settled in Pemberley, develops a strong mutual affection for Elizabeth. Elizabeth and Darcy are on the most intimate terms with the Gardiners and are grateful to them, as it was their tour of Derbyshire that helped them to come close together.

This final chapter provides a satisfactory close to the novel. Here Jane Austen emphasizes the social rather than the personal happiness resulting from marriage. Instead of showing the love relations between Elizabeth and Darcy, the protagonists of the novel, their continuing relations with other people have been referred to. We may now look back to the opening sentence of the novel and find that Darcy, a man in possession of a good fortune, at last gets his wife, although it is not his 'fortune' by which he gets her.

(*Chapter 61*)

5

The Title of the Novel : Its Significance

Jane Austen has given the title *Pride and Prejudice* to her novel after much deliberation. This will be evident from the fact that she originally named her novel, *First Impressions*, which was perhaps her first attempt at writing a novel. But fifteen years later, in 1813, she revised her novel and gave the new title, *Pride and Prejudice*, to it. This latter title and the theme of the novel are said to have been suggested to her by a novel (*Cecilia*, 1782) of a contemporary female novelist, Frances (Fanny) Burney (1752-1840).

Although the title *Pride and Prejudice* seems to be more appropriate than the first title, a few critics like F.W. Cornish are in favour of the first title. They hold that the original title is much more significant than the later one. For, in the story of the novel the first impressions play an important role. Elizabeth is misled in her judgment and estimate of both Darcy and Wickham and this leads to various complications in the novel. Her regard and sympathy for Wickham and her hostility and prejudice against Darcy are due to her first impressions about them. Darcy also is blinded by his lofty sense of aristocracy and makes a wrong assessment of Elizabeth's worth by his first impressions of her. Thus, it is because of their first impressions of each other that the two lovers are separated the moment they meet.

Thus, the importance of the first impressions of Elizabeth and Darcy cannot be denied. Yet, the name *First Impressions* does not bring out the true significance of the novel. It may seem to indicate the complications that will arise in the relation between Darcy and Elizabeth because of their first impressions of each other. It does not hold any clue as to how the complications can be removed. Darcy, the hero of the story, shows his haughtiness and pride on the occasion of his first meeting with Elizabeth, the heroine. He even discards her coldly by saying: "She is tolerable; but not handsome enough to tempt me; and I am in no humour at present to give consequence to young ladies who are slighted by other men" (Chapter 3). Elizabeth overhears him. Her vanity and self-respect are wounded. This creates a strong feeling of prejudice in her heart against Darcy. Thus, Darcy stands for 'pride' and Elizabeth, for 'prejudice.' Darcy is possessed by family pride and Elizabeth, by the prejudice that he is all pride. Then ensues a struggle of their mutual attraction against their mutual repulsion. Finally, both Darcy's pride and Elizabeth's prejudice are destroyed and they are united. The novel gives us an interesting account of the development in the hero and the heroine.

Darcy is very much conscious of his own worth and high social rank. So he looks down upon the people of a lower rank with a lofty condescension. This is particularly noticeable in his behaviour with the Bennets. And all the people of Longbourn also regard him as a man given to excessive pride. Yet, this proud man has fallen in love with Elizabeth, which he discloses in a party given by Sir William Lucas. There he tells Miss Bingley about Elizabeth: "I have been meditating on the very great pleasure which a pair of fine eyes in the face of a pretty woman can bestow" (Chapter 6). His better judgment rebels against this love for a social inferior, and he tries desperately to check it. But the love proves too strong for his reason and he proposes to Elizabeth at Hunsford. Love for Elizabeth has mellowed his pride. He tells Elizabeth: "In vain have I struggled. It will not do. My feelings will not be repressed. You must allow me to tell you how ardently I admire and love you" (Chapter 34). But he still maintains his aristocratic veneer. And this makes Elizabeth's prejudice against him continue and she summarily rejects his suit. This curt rejection by Elizabeth is a turning point in Darcy's career. He now realizes his folly. He is determined to relax a little of that pride which has been too inflexible so far. Thus, Darcy is transformed in a few months into a polite, self-forgetful gentleman, anxious to please and serve others. 'Pride', the first part of the title of the novel, thus gives way to love and understanding.

Elizabeth, who has developed her prejudice, has to cure herself of this weakness before she can be happy in life. Her dislike for Darcy is produced by his uncomplimentary remark about her on the occasion of his first meeting with her. Once this prejudice about Darcy is formed, Elizabeth is unable to judge him dispassionately. She soon meets Wickham who maligns the character of Darcy and this feeds her growing dislike for Darcy. This dislike is further strengthened by her suspicion that Darcy has been instrumental in ruining Jane's happiness by keeping Bingley away from her. When her hatred for Darcy is at the highest, Darcy proposes to her and she curtly rejects him accusing him of his meanness to Jane and Wickham. But a letter from Darcy brings her face to face with the truth. It is a mortifying experience for her to learn how utterly she has misconceived both Darcy and Wickham. She becomes gradually aware of the real merits of Darcy's character. Her regard for Darcy is increased by his role in the deliverance of Lydia. Thus, 'prejudice,' the second part of the title, is dissolved in love. Darcy, freed from pride, and Elizabeth, freed from prejudice, are now united together happily.

The title *Pride and Prejudice* also indicates a psychological tension between the hero and heroine. It is interesting to note that Darcy and Elizabeth become interested in each other almost as soon as the conflict between pride and prejudice begins. But both of them have intelligence and personality. Elizabeth firmly controls her emotions. She does not express her sentiment for Darcy. Darcy at first dislikes Elizabeth for her lower social rank and lower cultural level of her family. But he is gradually drawn to her against his will by her attractive personality. It is this conflict or psychological tension that paves the way to their final union. Darcy's gentlemanly qualities, civil manners and warmth of love conquer the prejudice of Elizabeth against him. And Darcy's pride is also humbled by Elizabeth's strength of character, intelligence and personality.

Thus, as 'pride' and 'prejudice' play an important part in the story of Darcy and Elizabeth, the protagonists of the novel, the title seems to be most appropriate. But, one may say that an exclusive preoccupation with pride and prejudice betrays a lack of artistry. It would then appear as a naïve recital of the plot of a morality play. Jane Austen's art, however, is too subtle to allow this to happen. The title is a mere vesture of a deep human problem which is unfolded in the novel. A.H. Wright justly observes: "To say that Darcy is proud and Elizabeth prejudiced is to tell but half the story. Pride and Prejudice are faults; but they are also the necessary defects of desirable merits; self-respect and intelligence." Moreover, the novel makes clear the fact that Darcy's pride leads to prejudice and Elizabeth's prejudice stems from the pride in her own perceptions. Thus, besides presenting a human drama of love, intrigue and marriage, the novel makes us aware of the danger that some rigid conceits like 'pride' and 'prejudice' may put us in. So, the title *Pride and Prejudice* has been most discreetly chosen by Jane Austen.

6

Pride and Prejudice : A Novel of Manners

The novels of Jane Austen are comedies in which she has presented a comic view of the social life of her time. These novels are appropriately called novels of manners, and the manners depicted in the novels are those of the eighteenth century English life. As a moralist Jane Austen worked in a narrow field. This narrowness of her range was due to the social milieu in which she lived. She never tried nor even attempted to write about the people she did not know or the place she never visited. She always confined herself to the 'small two square inches of ivory.'

Jane Austen was the daughter of a humble clergyman living in a little village. Except for short visits to neighbouring places, she lived a static life, but she had such a keen power of observation that the simple country people became living characters in her novels. The chief duties of these people were of the household. Their chief pleasures were in country gatherings and their chief interest was in matrimony. It is the small quiet world of these people free from the mighty interests, passions, ambitions and tragic struggles of life that Jane Austen depicts in her novels.

In this respect *Pride and Prejudice* holds a special position among her other novels. The most popular of her novels is the greatest as well, particularly for its presentation of English country society exactly as it existed in the eighteenth century. Jane Austen did for the English novel precisely what the Lake Poets did for English poetry. She refined and simplified it and made it a true reflection of English life. She made the 'dreary intercourse of daily life' the central theme of her novels. In *Pride and Prejudice* she pictured a limited part of the English scene. "Three or four families in a country village is," she said, "the very thing to work upon." Her small world is that of the provincial gentry. She leaves out many aspects of experience, but what she pictures is grounded upon so comprehensive a knowledge of human nature as to universalize it. Her men and women, true of their own period, are true also of all time. She stayed within the range of her imaginative inspiration. That range was almost of the same circumference as her own personal experience.

The life painted by Jane Austen in *Pride and Prejudice* was a life of the gentry in the countryside of England. It was a life of opulence, a life of quiet and enjoyment, a life uneventful, exempt from severe struggles and devoid of heroism, a life presenting no material for tragedy and hardly an element of pathos, a life in which matrimony was the chief incident and the most interesting objects were the hereditary estate and the heir. *Pride and Prejudice* deals with the upper middle-class society of rural England. All important characters, Mr Bennet, Darcy, Bingley, belong to the country gentry. Even Collins is a rector in possession of a parish whereas Lady Catherine is the owner of a rich manor.

The first thing we learn from a study of the novel is that the upper middle-class of the time had enough leisure. They were financially well off and could afford to have balls, dinners and other pastime of the type. In the novel we come across the balls at Meryton and Netherfield, dinners at Longbourn and Rosings, and frequent visits to the beauty spot, the Lake District. Much importance was attached to dress, manners, formalities, etiquette etc. These people knew the latest fashions of the day. Some of the conventions and codes of behaviour of the eighteenth century are remarkably presented in the novel. During those days women were forbidden by convention to move in any society other than the one in which they were born, and the small class of English gentry to which Austen belonged was particularly bound by this convention. Austen saw the folly, self-deception, irresponsibility, silliness, the individual's lack of knowledge of himself, of her own age and rendered them permanently in her novel.

The highlights of the eighteenth century rural life were little visits, morning calls, weddings, shopping expeditions, or the quizzing of new arrivals. The acme of excitement consisted of a ball, the most appalling social scandal and elopement. All these features of the eighteenth century rural life go to make up the plot of *Pride and Prejudice*. Life in the country seemed to flow almost in an uninterrupted way. Sometimes we come across in the novel a nostalgic suggestion of the elegances of a leisured age like, old-fashioned ceilings, white-panelled rooms gleaming with crystal lustres and carriages passing along the roads arousing curiosities of the villagers. But the greatest concern of the eighteenth century mothers in the rural side is the successful marrying of their daughters to worthy and moneyed grooms.

In *Pride and Prejudice* we find all the families in the neighbourhood of Netherfield and Longbourn, having daughters of marriageable age, entering into active competition with one another for the coveted prize of a rich son-in-law. Vulgar and uncivilized mothers like Mrs Bennet, who do not seem to be rare in the society, remain busy scheming, and in their passion to out-distance their competitors they even urge their husbands to force themselves on the notice of a rich young stranger so as to get on visiting terms with him. Walks, balls, tea and dinner parties are all arranged with due regard to their value in promoting matches.

In depicting this Jane Austen also presents the follies, whims, inconsistencies, meanness and thick-skinned vulgarity of the eighteenth century people, in her own ironic manner. The secret complexities of self-love, the many vanities, the quiverings of selfishness, the odious unawareness of the arrogant and the vulgar are all reflected in *Pride and Prejudice*. If Darcy is pride personified, then Elizabeth is prejudice. And to most of the eighteenth century provincial people such things as pride and prejudice were looked upon as disturbing factors strong enough to cause social tension.

Balls given by some rich patron are periodical events in the social world as presented by Jane Austen. These provide young ladies with great opportunities to come into the notice of rich bachelors. But it is by no means to be presumed that all rich bachelors are willing to be tempted by the allurements of husband-hunting butterflies. Social rank plays a very important role in this respect. Social inferiority carries with it its own stigma in the matrimonial world. Conventions and class-distinctions are adhered to with jealous care by social snobs and marriages between members of a humble rustic family like the Bennets and an aristocratic family like the Bingleys or the Darcys, are the exceptions rather than the rule.

The system of patronage is one of the features of the society pictured by Jane Austen. Silly old dowagers like Lady Catherine having livings to dispose of, dispense their favour to fools like Mr Collins who reward them in return with their fawning admiration. And while arrogant dowagers and stupid parishioners keep society amused, unscrupulous rakes like Wickham range about in search of romance and money. The camping of regiment in a small town like Meryton is a great opportunity for such rakes to abuse the ears of simple country girls and carry off their hearts. Thoughtless girls like Lydia lose their heads over such men and the liaisons usually lead to elopements.

It is thus seen that the world Jane Austen delineates in *Pride and Prejudice* is essentially the world of social pretension and ambition, of balls and visits, and speculation about marrying and giving in marriage, of the hopes and fears of genteel people of moderate means — a world which she turned into a microcosm of life in its social aspect. The eighteenth century rural life is realistically recreated in *Pride and Prejudice* in all its habits, tastes and appearances. The entire cross-section of the eighteenth century society is here: the clergyman, the foolish mother determined to find out a suitable match for her daughter, the silly and funny Lady Catherine de Bourgh, the proud and haughty Darcy, the silly and childish Lydia, the gallant and wicked Wickham, the scheming Miss Bingley, the foolish and garrulous Mrs Bennet, the beautiful but prejudiced Elizabeth and self-defensively offensive Mr Bennet. All these characters together constitute the nucleus of a world predominantly guided and governed by the ethos of the marriage-seeking business. In this provincial world all conceivable social advancements and lapses take place. Lydia's elopement with Wickham is one of the most sensational events of the world of *Pride and Prejudice*, as it was of the real life in the eighteenth century English society. Jane Austen presents in *Pride and Prejudice* the class structure of the English society in a miniature form and in this self-imposed task of hers she becomes eminently successful as a chronicler of the society of her own days. Hence, *Pride and Prejudice* may be called a belated specimen of eighteenth century novel of manners.

7

Treatment of the Theme of Money and Marriage

Mark Schorer in *Kenyan Review* (1956) affirms that the social settings in Austen's novels is one in which a feudalistic social order that does not know it is dying, and a bourgeoise or mercantile order that is not yet confident that it is quite alive, meet and conflict and sometimes merge. This conflict between the old aristocracy and the new middle-class with the gradual assimilation of the former by the latter, was a crucial social phenomenon in the world since the eighteenth century. In *Pride and Prejudice* Austen creates a little world which reflects this social background of the age. Contemporary materialistic pressures determine and modify the behaviour of the people in her 'little neighbourhood.' Regulations in particulars of etiquette dictate a constant sense of decorum at balls and in dialogue.

If we are to name Austen's major concern in this novel, it would undoubtedly have to be marriage in an acquisitive society. In the current social context the choice of a husband remains, for most girls, the single most important decision in life. The subject of courtship was central to Austen readers in the nineteenth century English society, because it involved both the social perpetuation of a family line through inherited property and the intermixture of social classes. The state of marriage was the *sine qua non* of tolerable existence, as Charlotte would be the first to remind us. The attitude is personified in Mrs Bennet preoccupied with the pressures of society imposed upon a woman of her class. To be settled comfortably after getting all her daughters married in wealthy houses, was a state indicative of middle-class happiness. The rest of the minor characters in the novel are mere caricatures of class consciousness, as is Lady Catherine de Bourgh with her vulgar condescension.

Marriage is the end of the novel, but it involves more than the conclusion of a simple love story. It was an important social concern of the time and Austen in her letters to her niece, Fanny Knight, has expressed fairly fully her views on the subject. She herself did not marry, but as she was one of a marrying family and as an onlooker, she saw most of the game.

Mrs Bennet's five unmarried daughters in *Pride and Prejudice* pose a problem akin to that faced by most women in Jane Austen's time. The relationships of Elizabeth and Darcy, Jane and Bingley, Charlotte and Collins, and Lydia and Wickham, are instrumental in developing the theme of money and marriage, with its social and economic implications.

Pride and Prejudice is primarily preoccupied with the business of match-making. And money plays an important part in it. David Daiches has written that Austen is the only English novelist who is, in a sense, a Marxist before Marx. She exposes the economic basis of social behaviour with an ironic smile. Money, however, is not different from, but part and parcel of marriage. The theme of Austen's novel is marriage into an economically superior society. Behind the match-making drama there is always the talk of provision. There are glimpses of resentment at the limitations of an economic world in which women had no future but what their husbands could provide, or their fathers, if they had been unlucky in the hunt. Jane Austen, being a realist, and a practical one at that, cannot ignore worldly considerations. Hence, *Pride and Prejudice* begins with: "It is a truth universally acknowledged that a single man in possession of a good fortune, must be in want of a wife," although the statement is ironical because the novel is more about the girls in search of husbands than young men in search of wives. And this brings the relatives of Darcy and Elizabeth, Lady Catherine and Mrs Bennet unexpectedly together, since both are venal about marriage and blind to its moral significance for the individual concerned. If we make this theme important we perceive that there is, after all, some sort of criticism in the novel. The progress of the two central couples towards matrimony shows what it ideally means. But for representative people of very different classes in society, it is a transaction involving merely money and status.

If Jane Austen meant to enforce the moral contrast between her ideal couples and her match-makers, it is strange that she allowed Elizabeth's intermittent reflections on the subject of prudent marriage to be so disconnected and so pointedly inconsistent. It is true that she is appalled by Charlotte's loveless marriage for financial security, but Elizabeth's readiness to condemn Charlotte operates more as a means of throwing light on her wavering judgment, than as an insight into marriage in society.

The marriage and money theme operates in an even more baffling way when Elizabeth herself comes to marry. Walter Scott has been teased for declaring that Elizabeth decides to marry Darcy because when she sees Pemberley her prudence begins to subdue her prejudice. Of course we are not supposed to take so literally Elizabeth's own joke to Jane that she must date her love for Darcy from her first seeing his beautiful grounds. The fact remains that Elizabeth does make, what, from the material point of view, is a glorious match and that its material splendour is pointedly put forward.

Elizabeth may make mistakes in analysing complex personalities, but she never surrenders her values for those of the society around her. For instance, she is pointedly ironic in her retorts to Wickham and Colonel Fitzwilliam, when they imply, on separate occasions, that she is ineligible for them on account of her comparative poverty. She is the only complex character in the novel with no social façade whatsoever. However, even she cannot be a rebel. She cannot contemplate the possibility of happiness outside her social sphere in which material wealth denotes moral well-being and a certain amount of prestige, too. This is betrayed in her half-awed, half-ironic utterance: "To be mistress of Pemberley might be something." The point is, Darcy without his property would not have been so readily considered an eligible bachelor even by her. At least she does discriminate between simple social types and individuals with free wills, and is decided that she must choose and marry a person who is undefeated by his social position and invulnerable to the pressures of society. Darcy is not, by any means, so worthy a person, but he is, at least, freer of social limitations than Wickham, Collins or Fitzwilliam. At least he does dislike social limitations and he does have a good taste and culture. It is only the imposed pride of rank and wealth that makes him behave with an obstinate over-confidence. Whatever it may be, both Elizabeth and Darcy can find no way out of a compromise with society, though both have airs of being individualistic and detached.

The Bennets are an example of an incompatible couple created by society, though the fault lies partly with the husband who probably submitted to a giddy impulse when he married, ignoring a rational approach to courtship. As a result he has to forego happiness for the rest of his life, for, his society has no respectable way out of a faltering marriage. As a man of means Mr Bennet must have been lulled into believing that any woman would suit for a wife, just as Mrs Bennet must have been taught that any man of means would make a desirable husband. However, Mr Bennet refuses to project a front of his own responsibility and continually uses his irony to upset the social order that has overwhelmed him permanently.

Charlotte provides an entirely different case. She accepts a foolish man without any desire, whereas Mr Bennet desired a foolish woman. Charlotte's is only a polite form of prostitution, sacrificing what is most valuable in the self, under economic pressure. She knows that she lives in a society that considers a penniless old maid more as an exasperating burden upon the family than as a subject for sympathy. The shadow of economic anxiety withers every other desire in her. Therefore, considering the pecuniary position of Collins, his character, connections and situations in life, she desires him without having the least attraction or love. Here Austen proves the opposite of what she has done through the Bennets, which is, that suppressing sensuality completely under cold reason is also not the correct solution.

Austen then returns to the previous extreme and again shows how harmful unrestrained sensuality can be. Wickham and Lydia are two such people; one employing his sensual charms for the purpose of seduction, and the other, thoughtlessly surrendering to her passions. Wickham, a complex personality, discards all scruples to use his charms, perhaps in the same way as Mrs Bennet did when she was young, but far more ruthlessly and calculatingly. Young girls like Georgiana, Darcy's sister, unknowingly fall a prey to him. But, Wickham, too, makes a mistake, since he is forced to marry Lydia to save the Bennets from dishonour. Wickham combines intelligence and sensuality shrewdly enough, but he is malicious and is willing to corrupt others to gain his own ends. Lydia possesses a quality that no one else in the novel does. She is unaffected by all the pressures of society. Unfortunately, however, this defiance is carried to excesses, since she does not care for the honour of her family either, and the way in which she exercises this defiance, eloping and living with her lover, was considered a taboo for respectable girls in her day.

The pressures of an acquisitive society have acted upon all the three complex characters, Wickham, Mr Bennet and Charlotte, who are individuals with free wills. But in all the three cases the mind has either not worked or if it has worked defectively, the depiction of sensual relationships was condemned by the nineteenth century English society. With Lydia, however, Austen concedes to bourgeois morality that regarded passion as socially unmanageable and indulges in some moralizings through Elizabeth who laments how little of true happiness could belong to a couple who were brought together because their passions were stronger than their virtues.

Marriage at the end of a conservative novel should be, and is, the fulfilment of a personal moral quest. An impulsive or mistaken protagonist, frequently someone whose first choice in love was rash, later uses sober judgment and external evidence to select a partner in marriage. The 'true' marriage which follows a close and sceptical analysis of the self is also the marriage which commits a couple to a responsible leading role in society. Jane Austen's heroines have a tendency to end up married to a clergy or a land-owner — the spiritual or the material leader of a local community. Unquestionably the marriage of Elizabeth and Darcy suggests all these traditional aspects. Both undergo the process of true criticism of the self through a correct, humbling assessment of another. Pemberley is significant in this inward process not because it means money and status but because it teaches Elizabeth that Darcy's taste is neither formal nor falsely adorned and hints at a future life of creative social involvement for both Darcy and Elizabeth.

Thus, though the novel is replete with money, wealth and prosperity, Jane Austen never suggests that love and marriage should be sacrificed for the sake of money. We have one of the finest statements on this theme in the unfinished sketch of her novel, *The Watsons* :

> To be so bent on marriage — to pursue a man merely for the sake of situations — is a sort of thing that shocks me! I cannot understand it. Poverty is a great evil, but, to a woman of education and feeling, it ought not, it cannot be the greatest — I would rather be a teacher at a school, than marry a man I did not love.

8

Irony and Humour in *Pride and Prejudice*

Irony is the soul of Jane Austen's novel. The comic aspects of life she presents in her novel are but the ironic aspects visible to good sense in its contemplation of erroneous judgments and bigoted or merely indolent persistence in error, of the contradiction between our desires and the good that we really desire. The themes that Miss Austen uses for her fiction are all ironic. Irony is the hall-mark of her style. But this irony is not merely a particular way of saying or creating things. It is not bound to any specific form. It is rather the expression of the infinite within a man who has at once a delicate, sensitive and subtle perception of the contrasts and contradictions with which human life is filled. Chaucer, Shakespeare and Lamb are not only humorous but also ironical, and so is Jane Austen. Miss Austen's tales are not laughter-provoking, but they have a rippling sense of pleasure behind them. Her humour is quiet, delicate, ironical. She is not a satirist, for, satire connotes moral purpose. Jane Austen never lashes human follies; she faintly arches her eyebrows and passes on.

Irony is a mode of speech in which the implied attitudes or evaluations are opposed to those literally expressed. Ostensible praise or approval that implies derision or disapproval is, however, more frequent than the converse form. Thus, irony is the art of expressing two meanings simultaneously : the obvious surface meaning and a hidden meaning. The basic feature of every irony is a contrast between reality and illusion.

Jane Austen makes use of irony at different levels. She makes use of it in her narrative style to uncover the incongruity, even contradiction, existing under the surface of harmony, thereby adding a rich subtlety and complexity to her style. She uses it also in her characterization to expose her characters' misunderstanding of others, as well as their own self-deception. Even her dialogues are full of dramatic irony. They have one interpretation for the speaker, and quite another for the reader who possesses more information than the speaker. Sometimes certain words uttered by a particular character, and certain situations get imbued with ironic implications in the light of what happens later in the novel. Her use of irony, therefore, lends compactness, clarity and subtlety to her narrative, depth to her characterization and a comic touch to her plot, keeping the reader titilated and amused.

Of all the novels of Jane Austen *Pride and Prejudice* makes us laugh more. "With the creation of Elizabeth Bennet, Jane Austen was vowed to comedy," observes Mrs Margaret Kennedy. The Bennets are a comedy themselves. It is, however, mainly in the minor characters that the sources of mirth lie in *Pride and Prejudice*. The story itself turns upon a stock eighteenth century plot — a misunderstanding about a character. The novel is full of errors, misunderstandings and cross-purposes. The very first sentence of the novel is tinged with humour and irony. The sentence runs as : "It is a truth universally acknowledged that a single man in possession of a good fortune must be in want of a wife." The obvious surface meaning of this sentence is what many, especially the mothers of marriageable daughters, want to believe. But it is certainly not a truth universally acknowledged. The contrary appears to be true in most cases. And what we read in the novel is that a single woman must be in want of a man with a good fortune. The moment we understand the implied irony of the first sentence, we are in the comic world of Jane Austen.

Most of the events and situations in the novel have been given an ironic twist. Irony being an instrument of revealing the difference between appearance and reality, is always a source of inspiration and amusement. It also gives very interesting twists to situations. Darcy remarks about Elizabeth that, "she is not handsome enough to tempt me," and soon after gets captivated by "a pair of fine eyes" of Elizabeth. Taking into consideration the imprudence of a marriage alliance with the Bennet family, Darcy removes Bingley from Netherfield, but makes the same alliance himself. Collins proposes to Elizabeth when her heart is too full of Wickham. Darcy proposes to her exactly at the moment she hates him most. Elizabeth quite emphatically tells Collins that she is not the type of girl who will reject the first proposal and accept the second, but this is exactly what she does in respect of Darcy. Elizabeth thought that her prospects of marriage to Darcy were blasted by the infamy of Lydia's misconduct, but the affair actually served to bring them together. Lady Catherine's intervention to check the marriage between Elizabeth and Darcy helps only to expedite it. Examples of this kind are numerous in the novel.

Irony of character is even more prominent in the novel than irony of situation. Elizabeth who prides herself on her perception and disdains Jane's blindness to the realities, is herself quite blinded by her own prejudices. Darcy always thought himself to be a gentleman, but his proposal to Elizabeth is quite ungentlemanly. Wickham is graceful to look at, polished and refined in his manners, but at heart he is an unredeemed villain. The Bingley sisters hate the Bennets for their vulgarity, but are themselves vulgar. The fact is that there are incongruities and contradictions inherent in human nature itself, and Austen portrays them for amusement and moral education of her readers.

It is not the characters alone, but the language of *Pride and Prejudice*, too, is most adequate to the author's ironic involvement in the novel. It is light, bright and sparkling. This is clear in our enjoyment of Mr Bennet's sarcastic humour when Mrs Bennet asks him to tell Elizabeth that she must marry Collins.

> Mrs Bennet rang the bell, and Miss Elizabeth was summoned to the library.
>
> "Come here, child," cried her father as she appeared. "I have sent for you on an affair of importance. I understand that

> Mr Collins has made you an offer of marriage. Is it true?" Elizabeth replied that it was. "Very well — and this offer of marriage you have refused?"
> "I have, Sir."
> "Very well. We now come to the point. Your mother insists upon your accepting it. Is not it so, Mrs Bennet?"
> "Yes, or I will never see her again."
> "An unhappy alternative is before you, Elizabeth. From this day you must be a stranger to one of your parents. — Your mother will never see you again if you do *not* marry Mr Collins, and I will never see you again if you *do*."
>
> (*Chapter 20*)

Another example of dramatic irony in dialogue may be found in chapter 43 of the novel where Mrs Reynolds, the housekeeper of Pemberley House, says that she does not know when her master, Mr Darcy, will marry, since, as she nays, "I do not know who is good enough for him." She is here innocently praising Darcy. But to Elizabeth's ears must be echoing Darcy's words: "She is not handsome enough to tempt me." Mrs Reynolds' observation in the light of these words of Darcy and his recent proposal to Elizabeth, get imbued with many ironic implications of which poor Mrs Reynolds must be totally unaware. One more instance will suffice to understand the peculiar blend of irony and humour in *Pride and Prejudice*. For a retrospect of Mr Bennet's married life Jane Austen admirably writes: "To his wife he is very little otherwise indebted than as her ignorance and folly had contributed to his amusement. This is not the sort of happiness which a man would in general wish to owe to his wife; but where other powers of entertainment are wanting, the true philosopher will derive benefit from such as are given."

In Jane Austen's diction, there is present a certain grandiloquence, that, being too heavy for the thought, casts a shadow of doubt on its veracity or validity. Sometimes just a single word adds dimensions to the whole speech. Mrs Collins and Mary's speeches abound in this kind of irony. Caroline Bingley writes to Jane: "If you are not so compassionate as to dine today with Louisa and me, we shall be in danger of hating each other for the rest of our lives." Or, when Collins speaks to Elizabeth: "In truth I must acknowledge that, with all the disadvantages of this humble parsonage, I should not think anyone abiding in it as objects of compassion, while they are sharers of our intimacy at Rosings." The heaviness of the words used by them ironically reflects upon the shallowness of the sentiment being expressed.

Irony in the hands of Jane Austen is always a means of rich comedy. She enjoys depicting the incongruities of character, but she does not allow them to taint the atmosphere of gaiety and mirth that fills the pages of her novels. Mrs Bennet's vulgarity drives away the suitors, but only temporarily. Lydia's thoughtlessness threatens irreparable disgrace, but ultimately her marriage with Wickham does materialize and the honour of the family is saved. It is interesting to note that it is the villainous character of Wickham and Lady Catherine, which is responsible for the union of Darcy and Elizabeth.

The irony of Jane Austen is not tinged with any bitterness, nor does it reflect her cynicism. It is amusing. It is the soul of her comedy. But it is not just verbal wit meant for entertainment alone. It provokes some deep thinking over some significant issues of human life. Professor Mudrick is of the view that irony is a neutral discoverer and explorer of incongruities. Of itself it draws no conclusions. But, neutrality is not an essential feature of irony. An ironist may be detached but not indifferent, withdrawn but not removed. Andrew Wright is justified in thinking that there is, in her, disengagement, an objectivity in her observation and depiction of the reality. She has her own ethos, her own set of values — whether adequate or not is entirely a different issue — and she makes her pronouncements on human activity with appreciable consistency. She criticizes marriages contracted for physical beauty or under economic pressures, and emphasizes the importance of love and esteem as the basis of a sound marriage. She explains the need of self-awareness. She ridicules hypocrisy and pretentiousness. Thus, irony, in her words, is "like the instrument of a moral vision" and not "a technique of rejection."

9

The Plot-Structure

The plots of Jane Austen's novels are extremely complex but Miss Austen shows an extraordinary skill in handling them. It appears that Miss Austen prefers a family with its many friends and acquaintances and she tries with her limited range to make things as complicated as possible. It had been well said that there is enough material in any of her six novels to serve a modern novelist with plots for two or three good sized stories. One story, one thread of narrative is not enough for her and the tangle of human relationship is never too intriguing for her.

Pride and Prejudice is an excellent example of a novel with a complex plot which Jane Austen handles most artistically. The plot of this novel has an exactness of structure and a symmetry of form. The plot of this novel centres round, as the title suggests, an eligible bachelor with family pride and a beautiful, young and unmarried girl with her prejudice for the pride of that handsome bachelor.

The plot of the novel is complicated by the fact that there are two young ladies in a small village courted by two young bachelors. The marriage of the two couples is thwarted by some obstacles, both internal and external. One of the obstacles is that the Bennets are a family having a much lower status than that of the families to which the young men belong. Besides, some vulgar members of the Bennet family including Mrs Bennet do their worst to drive these prospective husbands away. The elopement of Lydia, a daughter of the Bennet family, with Wickham makes the situation worse for both Elizabeth and Jane. Again, Miss Bingley also tries her best to thwart the love affairs of her brother and of Darcy. Besides these outward obstacles there are inner obstacles which are more important. Thus, Darcy is too haughty and outwardly repellent. He is proud and officious in hindering the progress of Bingley's affair with Jane. Again, Elizabeth is too quick to judge others and immediately develops a prejudice against Darcy. Bingley and Jane also are too pliant to be manipulated by others. At the end all these obstacles are overcome and the novel ends with the wedding-bells ringing for all.

Apart from this happy ending we are delighted to find the wonderful skill of the novelist in manipulating the plot. The plot of the novel has been described by a critic as a series of diverging and converging lines. Thus, the moment Darcy and Elizabeth meet they diverge because of their pride and prejudice. The movement of Darcy and Elizabeth away from each other continues to some maximum point when the lines begin to converge. The comic turn is indicated at the Pemberley meeting of the two lovers. Thenceforth the story moves rapidly towards the happy conclusion, although temporarily halted by the elopement of Lydia and Wickham. The clarity, neatness, simplicity and the symmetry of the plot movement are the most pleasing features of the novel.

Pride and Prejudice may be called a dramatic novel. Baker has rightly observed: "In *Pride and Prejudice* we have a dramatic subject treated dramatically." The dramatic tension of a gripping action-packed story with dialogues playing an important part is present throughout the novel. Some of the terms used by Aristotle in his *Poetics* to analyse drama are valid for some novels and particularly relevant to this well-constructed work of Jane Austen. According to Aristotle, a work ought to have a completeness or unity, that is, it should have a beginning, a middle and an end. *Pride and Prejudice*, indeed, has a definite beginning, a middle and an end. In her grasp of the logic of plot structure Jane Austen is a female Sophocles. The exposition starts with the meeting of Jane and Bingley, Elizabeth's strong prejudice against Darcy and Bingley's departure for London. The complication starts with the arrival of Mr Collins, his proposal to Elizabeth and her rejection of it, his marriage with

Charlotte Lucas, and Elizabeth's growing intimacy with Wickham. The climax is reached when Elizabeth rejects Darcy's offer of marriage at the Hunsford Parsonage and later realizes her mistake when she comes to know the true nature of Darcy and Wickham. The resolution starts with the sudden meeting of Elizabeth with Darcy at the Pemberley House, her changed attitude towards Darcy and Lydia's elopement with Wickham. The conclusion and denouement is reached through the marriage of Lydia with Wickham as a result of Darcy's earnest effort, Elizabeth's deepening affection for Darcy and acceptance of his proposal, and Jane's marriage with Bingley. The marriage of Elizabeth and Darcy is not merely a possible solution of the plot; it is as inevitable as the conclusion of a proposition constructed for geometrical demonstration. For a parallel workmanship one can look only to Shakespeare, to such a comedy as *Much Ado About Nothing*.

Dictated by the conventional three-decker manner of publication, *Pride and Prejudice* is very much similar to a three-act play. But, far more important than this is the resemblance of the novel to a romantic comedy, because Jane Austen has the same intricacy of sub-plots as Shakespeare and the dramatists of the Comedy of Manners. In fact, Austen's sub-plots are far better pre-planned than most of the sub-plots of the romantic comedies. This attempt to be immaculate in plot construction appears to have been inherited by Jane Austen from her neo-classical predecessors who insisted on the correctness of form.

There are five stories evolving concurrently in the novel. Before we name them it will be useful if we keep in mind a notable trait in Jane Austen, namely, her discrimination between simple and complex characters. There is a main plot concerning the love between Elizabeth and Darcy, both of whom are complex characters. Connected with this there are the sub-plots which are symmetrically balanced. As a foil to the main plot, acting in much the same way as the Celia-Oliver sub-plot in Shakespeare's *As You Like It*, is the secondary plot involving Jane and Bingley, who are both simple characters. The relation between plot and character becomes even more lucid when we come to the next two sub-plots which relate the stories of Lydia and Wickham, and Charlotte and Collins. In the former pair the man is complex, the woman, simple, while in the latter pair the conditions are exactly reversed. Noticeably the marriages of these two pairs are not regarded as successful. To clarify things further, Austen provides a fifth pair, this time already married, to act as a backdrop against which we can view and judge the other couples who get married in course of the novel. The Bennets are this fifth pair, the man complex, the wife simple.

From this basic infrastructure we can arrive at several different conclusions, just by noticing how Austen juxtaposes, compares and treats these five stories. The first thing that strikes us is that marriages seem to work only when both the partners are of the same mental type, as with Darcy and Elizabeth, and Jane and Bingley. For the simple reason that they are incompatible, the complex Charlotte, Wickham and Mr Bennet cannot communicate on equal levels with their partners. Lydia and Wickham have something in common, which is passion, but their minds are totally different. Theirs will not be a happy marriage. The moral to be derived from this need not be elaborated further. Perhaps, Charlotte and Lydia will realize this later, as Mr. Bennet already does, but, then perhaps, it will be too late.

The next thing that attracts our notice is the self-delusion that most people have about marriage itself. It takes the form of believing that marriage can be of passion, based on sensuality and nothing else, or of convenience, based on economic security. Lydia and Mr Bennet, we assume, believed in the former view. Lydia fell a prey to the sensual charms cunningly employed by a complex man, whereas Mr Bennet thoughtlessly surrendered to the seductive charms of a woman. Wickham, Charlotte and Mrs Bennet believed in the latter concept, Wickham wanting the money and the two women wanting the security their respective marriages could offer. But ideally, in a marriage, a person should search for a partner of a similar mental capacity, remembering that marriage is a matter of mutual give and take and cannot be based on selfish principles. This theme of marriage combines the various sub-plots of the novel artistically together.

It is interesting to note how Jane Austen deals with the

stories stylistically. We notice that the Elizabeth-Darcy story is told with surface romanticism and contains most of the verbal irony of the novel. The Jane-Bingley story is purely romantic. The Wickham-Lydia and Charlotte-Collins episodes are treated romantically with a solid foundation in social realism and with rather sordid and unhappy implications. The presentation of the Bennets with its implicit social realism emphasizes the consequence of indiscretion in entering into marriage. Thus, superficially *Pride and Prejudice* is romantic. On a deeper probing, however, we decipher the various levels of irony and if we stop to think a little, we will realize Jane Austen's serious concern with society and her extremely realistic outlook of life.

The action of the novel is clearly confined to the Elizabeth-Darcy episode. The Bennets remain static and the three other pairs progress quite simplistically with only one major reversal in the graph of each. Darcy's realization of his mistake gradually leads to a reconciliation between Jane and Bingley. Lydia's sudden elopement with Wickham ultimately leads to the marriage between Elizabeth and Darcy, and Charlotte's sudden acceptance of Collins's proposal leads to theirs. There are many more ups and downs in the process of Elizabeth's understanding of Darcy's personality — from initial dislike to attraction, from disdain to love and admiration. The process is shown with convincing minuteness, more so in the case of Elizabeth whose process of self-knowledge takes longer than Darcy's. The plot, besides bringing the two together, brings to each maturity and self-knowledge. Darcy's proud proposal is naturally rejected indignantly by Elizabeth — this being the nadir of their relationship — but his letter explains everything and henceforth, the way to their reconciliation is clear.

But, Austen is uncharacteristically clumsy from this point onwards. Darcy's proposal is flat. The Richardsonian letter is untypical of him and lacks credibility. For, the proud man is writing meekly to the girl who has rejected him unconditionally. Even worse is the novelistic technique of seduction as a suitable climax, which Austen also inherited from Richardson, but could not improvise a good substitute of it in any of her novels. This kind of threadbare revelation is too amateurish. There is a standard chase by an outraged father, a friendly uncle, and a now impeccable hero who makes devoted efforts to wed the scheming profligate Wickham to the innocent victim, Lydia.

In spite of these shortcomings *Pride and Prejudice* remains a marvel of construction because of the clarity, neatness, simplicity and the symmetry of the plot movement through a series of balancing events or incidents.

10

Narrative Technique

According to E.M. Forster the most important aspect of a novel is the story-telling aspect. But quoting Lubbock it may be said that the entire question about the method of craftsmanship of a novelist moves around the way a novelist narrates the story. The various methods of narration adopted by the novelist indicate the different viewpoints of the novelist.

A novelist may adopt different techniques of narration. Of them three are most common. Those are the direct or epic method of narration in which the novelist employs the third person narration, the autobiographical or the first person narration in which the narrator becomes one of the characters of the novel, and the epistolary method which presents the story through a number of consecutive letters.

The direct or epic method is the most common way of narrating the story. For, it has the advantage of flexibility on account of the narrator's assumed omniscience. This method was adopted early by Henry Fielding. He seemed to know all the characters and was endowed with a God-like vision of their motives and reactions. Jane Austen adopted this popular method of narration in her novel, *Pride and Prejudice*. Occasionally, she summarizes an incident or a series of incidents in such a way as to disclose certain reactions which could be known only to the omniscient narrator. Sometimes she poses as a historian in possession of all the facts, interested only in presenting them as they have happened; at other times she seems to pose as a neutral observer recording facts and disinterested impressions from what she is witnessing. Thus, sometimes she seems to be a chronicler of the past, and at others a narrator of the present.

But neutrality is, in fact, impossible for Jane Austen. For, she not only states the incidents and presents the characters, but also invests them with her own comments. Thus, at the beginning of the novel she comments on the characters of Mr and Mrs Bennet:

> Mr Bennet was so odd a mixture of quick parts, sarcastic humour, reserve and caprice that the experience of three and twenty years had been insufficient to make his wife understand his character. The mind of Mrs Bennet was less difficult to develop. She was a woman of mean understanding, little information, and uncertain temper... the business of her life was to get her daughters married.

Here, in a very economical compass, is an accurate sketch of both the characters drawn by someone who has a complete insight into them.

Again, Jane Austen shows herself as an omniscient narrator when she describes the entire reaction of the whole family of the Bennets and also of Charlotte Lucas when William Collins proposed to Charlotte Lucas and the proposal was accepted. The chapters in the novel (Chapters 22 and 23) where this reaction is described seem to be pieces of objective narrative by an omniscient writer who has identified herself with the viewpoint of the Lucases while maintaining the pose of an indifferent narrator. After Darcy's departure from the neighbourhood of Longbourn, Wickham freely tells the story of the former's wrong-doings to him — a story which he previously confided only to Elizabeth. While narrating this Jane Austen seems to know the entire situation and how the people of the neighbourhood received the story.

Jane Austen is, thus, ostensibly objective. But when she intrudes herself indirectly, she casts aside all pretence. While apparently proceeding along the lines laid out by the requirements of neutral narration, she often, by a word, a phrase or a personal note of qualification, discloses a view which cannot represent that of any of her characters and which may not be her own.

Jane Austen's very omniscience argues that a single point of view cannot comprehend the intent of the novel fully. The many shifts in viewpoint indicate a completeness and a detachment which none of the characters can possibly share. For instance, Elizabeth Bennet is unable to apprehend the true nature of Darcy's feelings for her until sometime after his own declaration of love. This declaration itself is a stunning surprise — but not to the reader who has already glimpsed the progress of the hero's feelings.

Jane Austen's distinct narrative method is revealed through the dialogue she uses to make her characters speak for themselves while she overhears them and narrates everything to her readers in the manner of a dramatist. Again, it is the dialogue that makes her narrative the most interesting and polyphonic in the Bakhtinian sense. Her dialogues are subtle, complex and revealing. The readers are often required to exercise their intellect to get at the significance of many an utterance in the novel.

11

Art of Characterization

The genius of Jane Austen as a novelist is best revealed through her wonderful capacity of portraying characters. In her novels we find a faithful portraiture of the society of the eighteenth century England. Her stories are as fresh and lively as in the days when those were written and her characters also are so built that they are sure to retain their brightness at any other time. They seem to be of real flesh and blood.

In her sketches of human nature Jane Austen is very subtle and delicate, but in depicting manners and customs she gives only broad outlines. On the whole her world is peopled with normal human beings. Her characters are neither exaggerated nor reduced to satirical proportions. They behave normally and act realistically. Macaulay ranked Jane Austen with Shakespeare. He said: "Shakespeare has had neither equal nor second, but among the writers who have approached nearest to the great master, we have no hesitation in placing Jane Austen."

Jane Austen has given us a multitude of characters, all in a certain sense commonplace, yet they are as perfectly discriminated from one another as if they are the most eccentric of human beings. This achievement stems from her ability to see life steadily and see it whole. She can see at the same time the surface of personality as well as the deeper roots of human behaviour and instincts. Thus, while viewing the individuality of her characters, she can also discern the causes and combination of qualities that go to make the characters what they are.

A sense of pervasive irony is also present in the characters of Jane Austen. The irony is betrayed in her portraiture of the characters of Elizabeth, Darcy, Collins, Wickham and others.

Irony is the soul of Jane Austen's comic view of life. It is the hallmark of her style. She recognizes the antithesis in human experience; the contrast between reality and appearance. This lends her ironical presentation of characters a distinct charm.

Jane Austen's world of reality is never disturbed for all its romances, elopements and seductions. Her characters continue to be normal even in the midst of grave provocations. Thus, Collins does not commit suicide in agony when his proposal is rejected by Elizabeth, rather he settles terms with Charlotte Lucas. Similarly, Darcy controls himself boldly and admirably after his proposal is rebuffed by Elizabeth. He explains himself to her and calmly waits for a change of her mind. There is, however, intense excitement in the dramatic ups and downs of the situations in the novel. But explosions are not merely averted but also turned into deeply amusing and pointedly acute evidences of human nature.

Jane Austen's characters present a nice and vivid picture of comedy of manners, because she is predominantly a comedian. Her first literary impulse has been humorous. She wants to make a thorough study of human follies and weaknesses. She wants to present a picture of life with all its mirth are gaiety. Her characters are psychologically drawn. Her picture of the weakness and strength of the human heart is complete.

Jane Austan's comic characters belong to a class of their own. Like Dickens, Jane Austen, too, has caricatures, but unlike Dickens they do not merely depend on a stock phrase or gesture, thus, becoming flat and wooden. Her comic characters are round and are shown from different angles. Besides, they have a definite role to play in the novel. They guide, to some extent, the course of action of some of the major characters. They are portrayed in such a manner as to make the satire in their portraiture not too blatant. In fact, she merely gives the picture, but leaves it to us to form our own judgment. Mr Collins, a distant cousin of the Bennet family, and Mrs Bennet are two of the humorous characters in *Pride and Prejudice*. They serve to heighten the progress of the story by contributing towards it in their own way.

Before Collins is introduced to us, we read his letter with which the writer prepares us for what is to be expected of him. When we first read the letter of Collins we notice the Latinized expression, the Johnsonese sentence structure, the pharisaical cliché and we are prepared to meet a pompous oddity and we wonder with Elizabeth — "Can he be a sensible man, sir?" The reply that Elizabeth gets from her father, "No, my dear; I think not. I have great hopes of finding him quite the reverse," is what we, too, expected. So, the first idea we get of him is that of an insensible man who says and does things which such a man should. He does not realize the impact it will cause on others and what reactions they will have when he says certain things so absurd, nor does he premeditate the consequences of his impulsive, stupid and insensible actions. He, thus, primarily is a product of Austen's youthful imagination in its most humorous mood.

When we meet Collins we realize the pomposity of the man who thinks highly of his position. He is a man, who because of his consciousness of his place as a rector, feels that he should set up the example for all that is good. Therefore, when asked to read from a novel, he takes up a sermon, thus boring the Bennet girls. Being a rector he feels that he should set up an example by getting married. Since it is not out of love that he wishes to get married, but merely to fulfil the wishes of his patroness, Lady Catherine, he first approaches Jane, the eldest of the Bennet girls. On being informed that she is going to be engaged, he immediately switches over to the next in line, Elizabeth. On being refused by Elizabeth he still is under the impression that Elizabeth would finally agree. For, he seems to be under the delusion that love has no part to play in marriage and a sensible girl only looks for a proper establishment in marriage. When he is informed by Mrs Bennet that Elizabeth is 'headstrong and foolish' he immediately gives up the idea of marrying her, for his patroness has advised him to marry a 'good and sensible' girl. His attempt is soon crowned with success. For, Charlotte Lucas, whose ideas about marriage are somewhat akin to those of Collins, agrees to marry him.

In Jane Austen's time rank played a very important role and those who possessed it looked down with lofty condescension on their inferiors. They not only expected their inferiors to treat them with deference, but also were done so. This aspect of social life is clearly shown in Collins's relation to Lady Catherine. Collins's individuality is lost in her presence and his obsequiousness and pomposity which are clearly evident, add to the humour of the character. He is ever ready not only to shower his compliments on everything in Lady Catherine's house, but also to comply with all her wishes. Again, as a rector he feels it his duty to advise Mr Bennet in his behaviour towards Lydia, who has brought disgrace to the family by eloping with Wickham, by asking him to forgive her, as a true Christian, adding that he should not allow her to return to his house again, making us wonder whether it is not merely a mockery of his position.

Collins, besides being a humorous character, has his own role to play in the novel. Had it not been for Collins, Elizabeth and Darcy could not have come together, as they do in the end. It was Collins who first gave the information of the engagement of Darcy and Elizabeth. On hearing this Lady Catherine comes down to Longbourn to find out the truth about this news of 'most alarming nature.' And it is her opposition that finally draws Darcy and Elizabeth together and they marry.

The other humorous character is Mrs Bennet who is no sooner introduced than she is defined: "She is a woman of mean understanding, little information and uncertain temper." The only aim in her life is to get her daughters married. By the end of the novel she does succeed in seeing her three daughters married, though it is to no credit of her own. She is indeed a woman of mean understanding as, though married for twenty-three years, she is yet unable to judge her husband, unable to grasp the digs at her. Her silly remarks and behaviour add humour to the novel. Her ideas are not guided by any prudence. She does not see the stupidity of Collins but tries to force her daughter to marry him, though without success. When Charlotte and Collins come, she imagines that they must be thinking when they will be in possession of the entail. When she gets the news of Lydia's elopement with Wickham, she does not see the fault in her own daughter, but blames her husband for having refused to go for a holiday, which would have then saved them from the disaster. When she hears of their marriage she does not seem to be in the least touched by the disgrace brought to her family, but goes on planning about clothes. She adds humour to the story by her contrivings of sending the carriage to bring Jane back from Netherfield, and on visiting Jane there declaring that she is still not fit to leave, in an attempt to make Jane stay close to Bingley for some time.

Austen's comic characters are thus fools and the humour is created by ridiculing them. It is through subtle irony that Austen ridicules these humorous characters who are not superfluous, but serve to heighten the plot and contribute to its development. They have been dealt with care and skill and they form an integral part of the main action of the novel.

Like the comic characters, the other minor characters in the novel have also received the careful attention of the novelist. In the novel besides the major pairs Darcy and Elizabeth, and Bingley and Jane, we have also the minor pairs like Collins and Charlotte Lucas, and Wickham and Lydia. Jane Austen has shown her eminence in the treatment of these minor characters. These characters are not only life-like, they have also been artfully incorporated into the story of the novel.

Mr Collins has been given the most entertaining role in the novel, *Pride and Prejudice*. He is the most egregious of the fools and the most laughable character we meet in the novel. He also serves three important purposes in the novel. We owe to him all that happens at Hunsford, the introduction of Lady Catherine and the further progress of the plot. As he is a near relation to Mr Bennet, he will inherit his property by entail after his death, as Mr Bennet does not have a male child. He depicts the picture of the servile domestic chaplain of the seventeenth century. Jane Austen's main purpose in depicting his character is to satirize the custom of patronage which on one side encouraged odious pride in the patron, on the other, odious servility in the dependent.

Charlotte Lucas, a friend of Elizabeth, is a sensible young woman of twenty-seven. Through her Jane Austen seeks to present the idea of marriage prevalent at that time. Marriage was a matter of security and Charlotte held that it was better to know as little as possible of the defects of the person with whom one was to pass one's life. So, when a solvent man like Collins proposed to Charlotte, she at once accepted it. Charlotte plays an important role in the novel in inviting Elizabeth to her house at Rosings where Elizabeth meets Darcy for the second time and it gradually changes the course of their relationship.

Wickham is the villain of the novel. He is painted as a wicked character who is deceitful, opportunist, hypocritical, lying and inconstant. He has a deceptively charming personality. So he easily wins the heart of Elizabeth and turns her mind against Darcy by his false accusations against Darcy. His deceit and hypocrisy do not last long. Soon Elizabeth learns from a letter of Darcy how unworthy and deceitful Wickham is. But, ironically, it is his villainy of eloping with Lydia that finally, draws the protagonists, Darcy and Elizabeth, close together. Thus, though a minor character, Wickham has not been kept on the fringe of the story but has been artfully drawn into the centre of it.

Lydia is the youngest daughter of the Bennets. She is a flirt who will never care to see how much defamation and ridicule her flirtation will bring on to her family. She is vain, ignorant, idle and absolutely uncontrolled. Her ignorance ultimately results in her elopement with Wickham because she does not foresee the implications of such an elopement. She is a victim of her passions. Jane Austen's purpose in introducing Lydia into the novel appears to have been her desire to throw some light on the society of her times. Lydia is also connected with the theme of marriage, which is one of the main concerns of the novel. Through her Austen has shown the evil effect of a thoughtless relationship based on passion, which sets off the ideal relationship of Elizabeth and Darcy based on true love and understanding.

The world of Jane Austen's experience was a very small one. She was a woman in an age when women were forbidden by convention to move in any society other than the one in which they were born. Further, she is one of the few women novelists who have accepted the limitations of their sex. She never describes a scene in which no woman is present. Her heroes are shown to us fragmentarily and with character and motives in part unexplained, as they appear to the girls with whom they come into contact. In every novel of Jane Austen there is one female character placed at the centre, who seems to represent the novelist herself and who is also an anxious spectator and judge of all that is going on around her.

The male characters in her novel, therefore, do not seem to have received equal justice with the women in their portrayal. Thus, Darcy is not wholly a coherent and credible fictional character. The change in his character is almost inexplicable. He first appears as a cold brutal snob and then suddenly changes into a decent character ready to do anything for Elizabeth. His coldness in the beginning does not balance with his warmth towards the end. For most part of the novel and especially in the first few chapters the reader is kept on the externals of Darcy. The novelist does not show us what he is thinking. Rather we see him only from Elizabeth's point of view, and that point of view is, after all, prejudiced. Mr Bennet lapses into indifference at the end of the novel. He is an example of a weak father. Mr Bingley is presented in the novel as a mere interesting contrast to Darcy. He approves of everything and everyone indiscriminately. He is arbitrarily enthusiastic and is so easily influenced that he abandons true affection on the advice of a friend.

Compared to the male characters the female characters in the novel appear more life-like, interesting and searching. Thus, Elizabeth, the heroine of the novel, appears to be a highly captivating figure. She is fairly attractive and genuinely desirable as a woman. She has a clarity of vision, a directness of purpose and a good sense. She has enough self-command not to be intimidated by Darcy or Lady Catherine. Her cleverness and strength gave her a feeling of natural superiority. She knows that she is more intelligent than others and she enjoys that conviction. She does not patronize Collins, but she sees the difference between herself and the clergyman very clearly. She is a keen observer and her observation of men and things is often more correct and appropriate than that of others. Her high spirit, ready gift of repartees and, above all, her admirable faculty for taking care of herself are enough to secure the basis of her character. Her sister Jane is also not a shadowy figure but life-like and impressive. She is the model of a sweet, simple, unspoiled village girl who charms everybody by her quiet and unassuming manners, her maiden-like coyness and her capacity for silent suffering. She is so lovable and charming that almost all the other characters in the novel have a very high opinion about her. Miss Bingley also remains conspicuous in the novel for her snobbery, intrigue and vulgarity. Lady Catherine is another character who seems to tower above all by her presence. Other women characters also appear quite distinct and they impress us by their peculiar personality.

There are three chief ways in which a writer may characterize his people. These are, description and comment, discussion by other characters and dialogue and action. Jane Austen has followed all the three methods in drawing her characters. Thus, at the beginning of the novel she allows Mr and Mrs Bennet to talk and then has a little paragraph of comment at the end of the chapter, in which she remarks that Mr Bennet is a mixture of "quick parts, sarcastic humour, reserve and caprice," and Mrs Bennet is "a woman of mean understanding, little information, and uncertain temper." Again, some interesting lights are thrown on the characters of Jane and Bingley by the discussion about them by Charlotte and Elizabeth, who hold contrary opinions about the pair. Jane Austen also adopts the third method in portraying most of the characters, especially Lady Catherine and Darcy.

In *Pride and Prejudice* there are some characters which are static and some which show interesting development. Instances of static characters are Mrs Bennet and Lydia. They remain at the end what they have been at the beginning. The characters of Elizabeth and Darcy, on the other hand, undergo important changes in the course of the novel. The characters of Jane Austen are not merely individuals, but universal, because she deals with the essential human nature which is the same in all ages. With her observant eye she has seen the great panorama of the society and presented it in her novel with an unerring insight.

12

Character–Sketches

Major Characters

Mr Fitzwilliam Darcy

Mr Fitzwilliam Darcy is the hero of the novel *Pride and Prejudice* not merely because he marries the heroine, Elizabeth Bennet, but because he plays a very important role and is the central figure in the plot of the novel. The most noticeable feature of Darcy is his pride and priggish nature, his supercilious attitude and his haughty mien, that partly go to form the title of the novel.

Darcy is a highly educated and cultured young man with a high and lofty sense of aristocracy. He is always conscious of his social superiority as a result of which he regards all others around him below his standard. Through him Jane Austen shows the evil effects of a money-ridden society on human character. Inherently and instinctively good and noble Darcy's attitude to society has been warped and twisted by his inordinate obsession with wealth and aristocratic status.

Darcy is out and out an aristocrat not only in his manner and feelings but also in his relations with his friends. As he notices that his friend Bingley is very much attracted by the charm and beauty of Jane, the eldest daughter of the Bennet family, he decides to take his friend out of this affair because he does not want that Bingley, being his friend, should enter into relationship with an ordinary family of the type of the Bennets. He is so definite about the infallibility of his judgment that he regards what he does to be the only correct and appropriate thing.

Darcy's general attitude towards the society is reserved and cold. His manners are proud and aristocratic. It is because of this that he becomes very unpopular at the first ball. He is so much reserved and cold that when Bingley introduces him to Elizabeth and asks him to take her as his dance partner, he refuses with the remark: "She is tolerable; but not handsome enough to tempt me; and I am in no humour at present to give consequence to young ladies who are slighted by other men." Thus, his manners are not inviting and he is continually giving offence.

We begin sharing our prejudice against him right from the beginning along with Elizabeth and nourish it till we reach the middle of the novel where Darcy is mocked by Fate when his proposal is curtly rejected by Elizabeth. It is from this point onwards that there comes a change in him and his nature begins to improve. False values have so long put his warm humanity under a shade. His true worth has been shunted to the background. But this has only been a temporary phase. What is genuinely good in him finally asserts itself when he really falls in love with Elizabeth. Given his moral and intellectual superiority, his struggle with himself to bring out his true self is bound to be acute and he gradually wins our sympathy.

Darcy has soon to realize that the standards of reason and aristocracy are not the only things by which a man is always ruled. Once he has removed his friend, Bingley, out of the circle of the Bennets so that he may not marry Jane, he finds that he himself is irresistibly attracted towards Elizabeth Bennet. But he is not quick to yield to this as he still remains highly egoistic and aristocratic. First, he tries to fight with his own self, but finding his sentiments and emotions stronger than his reason, he decides to disclose his love to Elizabeth with a hope to obtain her acceptance to his proposal. This is revealed in his words to Elizabeth: "In vain I have struggled. It will not do. My feelings will not be repressed. You must allow me to tell you how ardently I admire and love you" (Chapter 34). But to his utter surprise and regret Elizabeth refuses his proposal and this gives him a great shock. This poetic justice has a revolutionary effect on his aristocratic veneer and pride. This is the turning point in his career and his character assumes quite a different role henceforth.

Darcy's pride is hurt, but it has also a very salutary effect on him. The letter, which he now writes to Elizabeth explaining his position in reply to her accusation, is free from any demonstration of pride. It shows that a change is coming upon him. The next meeting between him and Elizabeth witnesses a great change in his behaviour. It is at Pemberley House that this change is visible. Elizabeth herself realizes this change in Darcy and as a result her attitude to Darcy is also changed.

The best in Darcy comes out after Lydia's elopement with Wickham. He now does a great service to the Bennet family once slighted by him. He goes out in search of the man who has always tried to defame him and his family. Not only this; he even goes to the extent of asking Wickham to marry Lydia, lest no slur might come on the Bennet family. His pride is thus, thoroughly subdued by love. The Lydia-Wickham episode serves only to call forth the deeper and nobler part of his character. What is more, after doing this great service, he does not want his name to be disclosed as the prime mover in settling the things. Nothing but the flame of ardent love for Elizabeth has prompted him to do all this selflessly. So, in the end he quite deservedly gets his prize. When he proposes for the second time, his proposal is readily accepted by Elizabeth. The very idea of marrying into a family that has been put to such shame shows that the last vestige of his false pride has been removed. Love, in the end, has triumphed and has wrought this change in his character.

Elizabeth in this novel tells Bingley that "intricate characters are the more amusing" (Chapter 9). And Darcy is an intricate character, most difficult to win and most worth winning. As a complex character Darcy along with Elizabeth is the model of the kind. Jane Austen has shown wonderful skill in dealing with and developing such a difficult character. In her usual quiet and competent manner she unfolds all the drama of cross-purposes and conflicts through which Darcy has to pass. The absorbing but at the same time amusing account of Darcy's development reminds us of a similar development of a great

Shakespearean character. It indeed goes to the credit of Jane Austen that a character who in the beginning looks like one who is most disagreeable and unpleasant, becomes in the end so noble and gentle that we begin to admire and love him.

Mr Charles Bingley

Mr Charles Bingley is one of the most important characters in *Pride and Prejudice*. Of course, his role is to play as the lover of Jane and our interest in him is mostly confined to his relationship with Jane. Apparently, in importance he is next to Darcy. He is a perfectly amiable, rich young man having an annual income of five thousand pounds. He is an attractive person capable of being loved for his own sake. He is a very free and unreserved young man with a charming personality and polished manners. Thus, he is a striking contrast to his friend, Darcy. He has an invincible gusto for the good things of life and his desire for the joys of social life leaves him no time to apply those moral standards which are the obsession of Darcy. Jane Austen herself remarks about Bingley: "He was quite young, wonderfully handsome, extremely agreeable," and that he "was good looking and gentlemanlike; he had a pleasant countenance, and easy, unaffected manners" (Chapter 3). Jane's first impression about Bingley also testifies to these qualities of the young man. She tells Elizabeth: "He is just what a young man ought to be ... sensible, good humoured, lively and I never saw such happy manners! — so much ease, with such perfect good breeding (Chapter 4)!" Elizabeth also agrees with her and remarks: "His character is thereby complete."

Bingley is extremely modest and is somewhat irresolute. This lack of resolution and of strength of personality are evident when at the insistence of his friend, Darcy, and his sister Caroline he leaves Jane and goes to London. Bingley is so generous and unselfish that he avoids caution and calculation in his dealings with others. Thus he is weak-willed and is easily dominated by others. He depends too much on Darcy, even in matters so vital as love and marriage. He allows his friend to decide what is good for him and suspends his courtship of Jane at that friend's objection and resumes it only when that friend gives him the permission to proceed. Of course, we should not call Bingley a spineless person for that. For, Darcy has to convince him that an alliance with the Bennets will be imprudent for him. Besides, Bingley has to be further assured that Jane is indifferent to him and as such she will suffer no disappointment if he stays away from her. These circumstances exonerate Mr Bingley from a part of the blame for relying on a friend's judgment in the matter of his own marriage. Besides, even while submitting to his friend's guidance, he does not permit himself to be insincere. He suspends the courtship of Jane on Darcy's advice, but he refuses to be led into another love. He remains utterly indifferent to the charms of Darcy's sister. He genuinely loves Jane. When Jane falls ill at his house at Netherfield, he is much concerned and takes every care for her recovery.

Bingley is extremely social. He is fond of giving parties and holding balls at his house. There he invites his friends and relations to participate. He spends lavishly on these occasions to entertain his guests. We may have an idea of this from the novelist's account of the Netherfield ball. Bingley is an expert dancer. He dances with Jane twice at the first ball. He is thus very popular in such gatherings.

Bingley does not very much influence the progress of the novel, though his leaving of Jane, initiated by Darcy, affects Jane, Elizabeth and Darcy himself. Instead, he offers an interesting contrast to Darcy who is temperamentally poles apart from him. The simple and docile Bingley serves as a foil to the complex and authoritative Darcy. Bingley also highlights Wickham's false charm by his own genuine kindness. He indirectly throws some light on Elizabeth's character when Elizabeth tries to defend him. Again, in his romantic love for Jane we realize the true worth of the relationship of Elizabeth and Darcy.

Elizabeth Bennet

Elizabeth Bennet is the heroine of the novel *Pride and Prejudice*. She is the second of the five Bennet sisters. She is gay, charming, attractive intelligent and a keen judge of human nature. She has a lively and playful disposition and a challenging temper. Even such a fastidious critic like Saintsbury was forced to acknowledge the charms of her personality and the grace of her manners. Taking into consideration the various qualities of her character and especially the unusual vigour of her mind, it appears that the novelist has created this character almost exactly in her own image. Elizabeth is endowed with a beauty which is not very striking but which at once impresses us. Her most fascinating features are her eyes. We may remember that the enchantment of Darcy began when he discovered Elizabeth's fine eyes.

Elizabeth's attractiveness does not rest merely on her physical charm, but on the extraordinary liveliness of her mind. She possesses an independence of mind and thought. She has as much keen insight as an intelligent man of her age. The natural vigour of her understanding is such that her observations of men and things often go deeper than those of others. When even the shrewd Mr Bennet fails to foresee any danger in sending Lydia to Brighton, she alone is clear-sighted enough to warn her father solemnly against the indiscretion of such an attitude. This warning is based solely on her correct estimate of her sister's character and temperament. Later events show how far she is justified in her misgivings.

Elizabeth is the most talented of all the Bennet girls. She is so intelligent that she can easily understand that the Bingleys are not as good as her sister Jane has made then to be, and especially, Miss Bingley, who appears to her as a very cunning and proud lady. And she is correct in her assessment. Bingley and his sister leave Netherfield without giving any formal information to them and later on, Jane herself experiences the rude behaviour of Miss Bingley when she is in London staying with her uncle and aunt.

Elizabeth is a self-respectful young woman of many qualities. At Meryton ball she is only next to Jane in dancing and in impressing the assembly. Her performance at the ball is commendable. She is alert in her mind and heart. She overhears the talk between Darcy and Bingley at Netherfield, in which Darcy belittles her by saying: "She is tolerable; but not handsome enough to tempt me; and I am in no humour at present to give consequence to young ladies who are slighted by other men." This is enough to hurt her dignity and she does not forget this when the next time Darcy asks her to dance with him, and she declines the offer. She is well-behaved and polished in her manners. Even in expressing her likes and dislikes she is quite dignified. She rejects the offers of Collins and Darcy politely but firmly. Particularly, in the case of Darcy, when her mind is bubbling with prejudice against him, she does not allow her inner feelings to take shape in her words. She feels pity and sympathy for the shock that would overcome Darcy after her refusal, modestly thanks him for the honour that he has done her by proposing marriage and then politely declines the offer.

The character of Elizabeth is one of sacrifice and affection. Her love and affection for her sister Jane is exemplary and admirable. She is prepared to sacrifice everything for her. The moment she hears of Jane's illness, she immediately hurries to Netherfield and there she is in Jane's service day and night caring but little about her own comforts. Again, when Bingley leaves for London, perhaps with no hope of returning, her pain is no less than that of her sister who has been thinking of marrying Bingley, and when she comes to know that Darcy has been instrumental in detaching Bingley from Jane, her prejudice against Darcy reaches a high pitch. Any other girl in her position would have certainly accepted the offer of marriage of so rich and highly placed a man as Darcy, but she rejects the offer because of his part in ruining the happiness of her sister.

Elizabeth appears to be quite susceptible to prejudice in the beginning. But at the same time she is also flexible and resilient and capable of making amends. When she comes to know of Darcy's innocence, she changes her attitude towards him and slowly but steadily begins to love him. Thus, she is not correct in her first impressions. She blunders in judging both Darcy and Wickham. But the moment she realizes her mistake she is so sad and pained that tears begin to stream down from her eyes and ultimately she falls ill. She, however, mistakes in regard to those who are in close proximity to her. It is only when she distances herself from them and is able to judge in a cool manner, that she can distinguish the noble from the ignoble and the virtuous from the vicious. Thus, prejudiced as she is, she does not allow her good sense to be completely overshadowed by it.

Elizabeth possesses an unfailing wit and humour. In this respect she betrays the strong influence of her father on her character and temperament. Mr Bennet is witty and a master of repartees and so is Elizabeth. But, unlike her father who is sardonic and cynical, Elizabeth is always lively, vivacious and delighted with life. Even when her prejudice against Darcy has been roused most, she retains her calmness of temper and exemplary courtesy. Her witty remarks and repartees, though showing her dexterity in verbal fencing, are extremely enjoyable. Her only fault in this respect is that her usual assertive and unyielding nature makes her remarks at times appear impertinent. But the fact is that, in her Jane Austen has created an unconventional young heroine who, living in the world of sensibilities, is yet endowed with an almost unfailing common sense and independence of temper and attitude. This, in no small measure, adds to her charm.

Dr Bradley in his careful survey of Elizabeth's character has shown that nowhere, except probably at the Netherfield ball where Elizabeth talks rather boldly to Darcy about his character, does she say anything that passes beyond the limits of courtesy and decorum. Her high spirit with her perfect command of epigrammatic expression, her ready gift of repartee and, above all, her admirable faculty for taking care of herself are the qualities that make her so attractive. It would not be exaggerating to say that *Pride and Prejudice* is the story of Elizabeth and Elizabeth is the most brilliant creation of the novelist.

Jane Bennet

Jane Bennet is the eldest daughter of the Bennet family. She is twenty-two at the beginning of the novel. She is the model of a simple, sweet, unspoiled village girl, who charms everybody by her quiet and unassuming manner, maidenly coyness and a capacity for suffering mutely under the impact of the most cruel emotional disappointment, although she is not as gifted with intelligence and foresight as her sister Elizabeth. She has physical charm and is indeed the best-looking girl in the neighbourhood. There is attraction in her personality, beauty in her looks and grace in her manners. She has the patience, forbearance and meekness of an angel. Almost all the characters in the novel love her and have a high opinion about her. She is the favourite of her mother. Her father has the highest opinion about her judgment and good sense. Elizabeth simply dotes on her. Mr Bingley falls at once a prey to her charms. Even Darcy and Miss Bingley, who are highbrow and fastidious, recognize her merits. Mrs Hurst, Bingley's sister, calls her a 'sweet girl.' Jane is also an expert dancer and because of this she becomes the centre of interest at the Meryton ball. Bingley dances with her twice.

Jane is full of the natural womanly qualities of modesty and shyness. She loves Bingley sincerely, but she hardly expresses her love in words, so that Bingley, at some point, is not sure and certain of her love. But she is a true lover and so continues to love Bingley even when he appears to be out of her reach. She is so genuinely good-natured that she does not for a moment suspect Miss Bingley as instrumental in separating her brother, Mr Bingley, from her. Her unflinching faith in human virtue, makes her a refreshing contrast to Elizabeth who is often eager to believe ill of others. Her perfectly candid mind can never harbour any prejudice, for which she may have to regret later on. Thus, although she has got almost overwhelming proofs of Miss Bingley's insincerity and treachery she refuses to have any ill feeling towards her.

The most distinctive quality of Jane's character is her forbearance. She is always inclined to think and believe the best of others. Her faith in the nobility of human nature is unshakable and whenever any charge is levelled against any deceitful character, she becomes extraordinarily zealous in his defence. After the first ball when everyone joins in openly criticizing Darcy for his haughtiness and pride, it is only Jane who speaks words in his favour. The same thing is repeated when the devilish nature of Wickham is exposed. Of course, she is in a fix this time and does not want to disbelieve either Darcy or Wickham.

So, she agrees that whatever Darcy has written about Wickham might be the result of some misunderstanding. "Interested people have perhaps misrepresented each to the other," she observes.

Jane is so utterly docile, meek and self-effacing that she is hardly left with any individuality. In fact, a perfect man or woman is essentially a colourless and uninteresting character. Yet the sweet presence of Jane in the novel fills the novel with a sweet aroma of pleasantness. She has a great regard for her parents. She is a great friend to her sister, Elizabeth, and the two confide their secret thoughts to each other. She is a dutiful and supportive daughter, taking full responsibility for the family during Lydia's elopement.

With Bingley, Jane represents romantic love, which is seen in the novel as unrealistic and suspect. It is Jane's sweet nature, hiding her vulnerability, which leads to her being misunderstood and the loss of Bingley for a while, with all the consequences on the relationship of Darcy and Elizabeth. Through Darcy, finally, everything is resolved, but we still see that it is only because Jane is so good a person that her romantic relationship works. Jane is a contrast to Elizabeth, but she also complements Elizabeth as Bingley does Darcy. At the end of the novel, it is Jane and Bingley, who join the hero and the heroine in Derbyshire as true friends and as, indeed, 'good' characters.

Minor Characters

Mr Bennet

Jane Austen reveals her mastery in the art of characterization in her portraiture of Mr Bennet, the head of the Bennet family at Longbourn. With a few masterly strokes of her brush she has been able to produce the concrete appearance of a person who remains almost in the background of the novel. Mr Bennet is a country gentleman with an income of two thousand pounds a year. He has five daughters and no son, and so his estate is entailed to his nearest relation, a cousin, Mr Collins. He has married in his youth a woman of weak understanding and illiberal mind, being captivated by her youth and beauty, and for this act of youthful folly he repents later in life. His personal library is the place where he feels most at home and for the major part of his presence in the novel he remains there. Thus, he has been almost cut off from the rest of the family. Jane Austen, from time to time, brings him out of this sanctuary of his library just to enable us to hear a few of his typical cynical and humorous utterances. At the very outset she has introduced Mr Bennet with the description: "Mr Bennet was ... a mixture of quick parts, sarcastic humour, reserve, and caprice."

As Mr Bennet is endowed with a prodigious sense of humour, he looks upon the society around him as the natural prey of his wit. The follies and absurdities of others provide him the amusement he needs. Particularly, the follies of Mr Collins keep him in continuous good humour and mirth. This love for amusement often makes him seek for it in places which he should avoid. It is the silliest behaviour of his wife and younger daughters from which he derives his mirth and for this purpose he indulges in the heartless game of teasing them. But making his wife the butt of laughter and ridicule naturally has a pernicious effect on his own daughters who become disrespectful to their parents.

Mr Bennet's jokes and witticisms are tinged with malice and even cynicism. When he comes to know of the sudden illness of Jane because of an exposure to rain, which is the result of a deliberate act of Mrs Bennet of sending Jane on horseback to Netherfield, so that being ill she may remain with Bingley for a long period allowing Bingley to fall in love with her, he tells his wife: "Well, my dear ... if your daughter should have a dangerous fit of illness, if she should die, it would be a comfort to know that it was all in pursuit of Mr Bingley, and under your orders" (Chapter 7). Mr Bennet's ironical thrusts are, thus, sometimes extremely devastating. His masterpiece in this species of wit is the letter he writes to Mr Collins who has just warned Mr Bennet that if Elizabeth should happen to become engaged to Darcy, she will forfeit the good opinion of Lady Catherine for ever. Now, as soon as Elizabeth becomes engaged to Darcy, Mr Bennet writes the following note which is as concise as it is admirably sarcastic: "I must trouble you once more for congratulations. Elizabeth will soon be the wife of Mr Darcy. Console Lady Catherine as well as you can. But, if I were you, I would stand by the nephew.

He has more to give" (Chapter 61). The most delicious part of this sarcasm is that it would have been entirely lost on Mr Collins.

Mr Bennet is somewhat philosophical in the sense that he cares little about the world around him. He is not worldly-wise. His practical inefficiency is quite amazing. His imprudent marriage, his error in not saving up a capital out of his ample revenue in his youth when he was not burdened with a large family, his inability to foresee any danger in sending Lydia to Brighton and his utter helplessness when engaged in the task of searching out the eloped couple, go to show that he is a mere unpractical inefficient man of the world fit only to be a spectator of human life. His approach to life and its varying problems is light-hearted and non-serious. He has the capacity to laugh even on the so-called problems and awkward situations of life.

Mr Bennet is a simple and plain type of man. He is good-natured, harmless and a loving father. He is pleasant in his manners. He is seriously disturbed after Lydia's elopement and considers himself responsible for all that has happened. He leaves Longbourn with a firm determination not to return unless he is able to trace out Lydia. This is for once he becomes serious and active. It is frustration and disappointment for choosing a wrong partner of life and imprudence in not making adequate savings in time that have turned him into a cynic and recluse.

Mr Collins

Mr Collins is the rector of Hunsford Parsonage and distant cousin of Mr Bennet. He is stupid, pompous and conceited. He is, for all practical purposes, a clown. He is tall and stately. His air is grave and manners are very formal. But with all this he possesses an extra amount of absurdity which is always in advance of what one can possibly imagine. This is particularly revealed in his letter to Mr Bennet on hearing the news of Lydia's elopement. In this letter he expresses his full sympathy for the unfortunate family. Then he goes on to explain in no unmistakable terms his fear that the misconduct of one daughter is sure to prove injurious to the fortunes of the others, and he concludes by congratulating himself on having narrowly escaped allying himself with the family. He finally advises Mr Bennet, "to throw off your unworthy child from your affection for ever" (Chapter 48). Such is the Christian attitude of a curate to a man in distress! We are really shocked to find his lack of Christian charity as revealed in his letter.

Collins is not at all a sensible person. This becomes obvious to Elizabeth from his first letter to Mr Bennet. He has received little education and has little opportunity of moving in society. The influence of his dominant father on him has turned him into a very sheepish and slavish type of man. He is a mixture of pride and obsequiousness, self-importance and humility. It is because of his great veneration for Lady Catherine and his own conscious superiority as a clergyman that he has developed into such a mixture of opposites.

A remarkable thing about Mr Collins is his great regard for Lady Catherine. She is the symbol of human perfection to him. Collins thinks of her and her grandeur even when making love to Elizabeth. Quite insignificant objects become transformed in his eyes into something grand on account of their connection with Lady Catherine. The sight of Lady Catherine's phaeton passing his gate becomes a beatific vision in his eyes and a dinner at Rosings becomes transformed into a heavenly banquet. He looks on her as though she were dressed in a light that never was on sea or land.

Mr Collins is made of such oddities that he bores every body but is bored by none. Everybody wants to avoid his company. In making love and proposing to a girl he is as absurd as he is in his social behaviour. He gives long speeches as if he is lecturing to an audience. Brevity and seriousness are qualities he is completely unfamiliar with. His expressions are bristled with cliché. Thus, when proposing to Elizabeth he says, after giving a very long lecture about the reasons for his decision to marry: "And now nothing remains for me but to assure you in the most animated language of the violence of my affection" (Chapter 19). In his letter to Mr Bennet after Lydia's elopement he writes: "No arguments shall be wanting on my part, that can alleviate so severe a misfortune; or that may comfort you, under a circumstance that must be of all others most afflicting to a parent's mind" (Chapter 48). The orotund language in which this pompous prig speaks and writes is highly comical and betrays, in no small measure, his clownishness.

Mr Collins is fickle even in such serious matters as love and marriage. Marriage to him is not a matter of heart but a matter of necessity. It is necessary because he has a house, a service, a social status and particularly because Lady Catherine has asked him to marry. So, he starts with Jane and finally ends with Charlotte Lucas. In between he approaches Elizabeth who curtly rejects his proposal out of sheer disgust although Collins foolishly thinks that her rejection is due to her modesty. He seems to have no sense of honour and prestige. Thus Elizabeth's refusal and Darcy's indifferent behaviour have but little effect upon him.

But with all his shortcomings and idiosyncrasies Mr Collins has a few good qualities. He is orderly and systematic in the management of his house. He practises punctuality as an art and he proceeds in all his undertakings strictly according to his plan. He woos and marries by the calendar. He also believes in formalities and etiquette. He is equally prompt and equally formal with his congratulations and condolences. We cannot, therefore, dislike such a character. Jane Austen's main purpose in depicting this character is to satirize the custom of patronage, which encouraged on one side odious pride in the patron and on the other odious servility in the dependent. But it appears that she gradually rose far above her original intention and has succeeded in giving us genial humour where she only intended satire. Besides, Collins plays an important role in the novel in furthering the progress of the plot. For, it is Elizabeth's visit to Hunsford that brings her and Darcy close together, gradually paving the way to their final union in the end.

Mr Wickham

Mr Wickham was the son of a respectable gentleman who served for many years as the steward of the Pemberley estates. He was almost of the same age as Fitzwilliam Darcy's and had been the latter's playmate from his childhood. Darcy's father loved Wickham and was almost like his godfather. He supported Wickham at school and later at college. He intended Wickham for the Church and made in his will provision for a church-living to be bestowed on Wickham. He also left Wickham a legacy of a thousand pounds. But unknown to senior Darcy, Wickham grew up to be a wild and dissipated young man. After the death of his father Fitzwilliam Darcy succeeded to his father's estate. Then Wickham, who had finished his college education, expressed his desire not to take holy orders but to study law. Darcy was generous enough to pay him not only his legacy of a thousand pounds but also a considerable sum of money in lieu of church-living which he was not obliged to give Wickham.

The study of law, however, was a mere pretence. What Wickham really wanted to do was to pursue a life of pleasure in London. Soon he squandered away the money given to him by Darcy and then shamelessly applied to Darcy for a church-living which was then vacant. This time Darcy turned down his request and refused to have anything more to do with him. This enraged Wickham who now began to scheme of doing some lashing injury to him. He thought of entrapping Georgiana, Darcy's sister, into marriage with him, which would make his fortune and at the same time gratify his feeling of resentment against Mr Darcy. With the help of Mrs Younge, a companion of Georgiana, he became intimate with Georgiana and managed to persuade her to elope with him. Wickham would have carried out the nefarious plan, had not Georgiana disclosed the matter to her brother who took immediate steps to remove his sister away from Wickham's reach. Soon with the help of some friends he obtained a commission in a regiment stationed at Meryton and in no time we find him spreading his charm on Elizabeth, and being unsuccessful with her, finally, eloping with Lydia.

Thus, Wickham appears in the novel as a deceitful, opportunist, extravagant, hypocritical, slanderous and inconstant person. He may be called the villain of the novel. He has a handsome, charming and stately figure and can easily impress anybody by his impressive personality and suave and pleasing manner. So he can easily become intimate to Elizabeth. He is intelligent and shrewd. He learns that Elizabeth bears some prejudice against Darcy. So, he begins to malign Darcy's character to her by narrating to her some false stories about Darcy making her believe that Darcy has treated him most dishonourably and deprived him of his legitimate share in the property of Darcy's father. Further, to gain the sympathy of Elizabeth he fabricates to her that in order to have some earning and a position in the society he has been obliged to accept the military service. Elizabeth becomes so much fascinated by Wickham that her aunt, Mrs Gardiner, thinks it necessary to warn her against the imprudence of contracting marriage with him, who, however, desirable otherwise, has not a penny in his purse. But this warning does not abate Elizabeth's enthusiasm for Wickham. Elizabeth comes to her senses when she hears of Wickham flirting with a rich girl, Miss King, learns from Darcy's letter about his true character and finds him eloping with her younger sister Lydia.

Wickham is inconstant in love. He considers the girls a means to satisfy his sensual desires. So, he first chases Georgiana, then Elizabeth, then Miss King and finally, Lydia whom he is compelled to marry. In marrying Lydia he also has made his bargain. He is shameless and his shamelessness is evident when after his elopement he comes to Longbourn. There he behaves in a manner as if nothing serious has happened. No sign of repentance is there on his face for having done so immoral a deed.

It is interesting that Wickham who seems to be so active, affecting so many people's lives, actually appears very seldom in the novel. His confrontation with Darcy and the subsequent revelations to Elizabeth are followed only by two short, if significant, conversations with Elizabeth, the reported elopement and a brief welcome and farewell at Longbourn. His main role in the novel is to help us understand Elizabeth, and to change her by her realization of what he really is. Although not directly, yet it is through Wickham that Elizabeth realizes her own lack of good judgment, her prejudice, her susceptibility to flattery. Wickham shows us Elizabeth's romantic side and also provides a rival for Darcy. He also shows us Elizabeth's capacity for prejudice. The key scene occurs in chapter 16 where, on first acquaintance, Wickham pours out his self-pitying tale about Darcy. He is careful to test the strength of Elizabeth's bias first, then presents a clever story designed to stir sympathy and belief. He plays on her credulity twisting the essential truth so that he appears in the best light, and Darcy, as proud and in the wrong. Wickham also demonstrates public prejudice. Everyone agrees he is charming until the elopement, when they as unanimously condemn him. Wickham's marriage is vital to the plot not only because it brings Elizabeth and Darcy together, but because it also represents what is in the end the wrong sort of marriage. But although he is important for the development of the plot, he is, in reality, a vicious, worthless man.

Mr Gardiner

Mr Edward Gardiner is the brother of Mrs Bennet. He is settled in a respectable line of trade in London. He is educated, well-bred, agreeable and a kind-hearted gentleman. He is very affectionate towards his nieces. He is the proverbial good Samaritan of the Bennet family. His regular Christmas visits to the Bennets are harbingers of great joy to the Bennet sisters, especially to the eldest two.

Mr Gardiner is a shrewd judge of human character. His impressions of Wickham and Darcy are substantially correct and they in no small measure help the process of Elizabeth's change in her attitude to Darcy. His praise of Darcy and condemnation of Wickham have a profound effect on Elizabeth. Thus he has an important role to play in the development of the main plot. By taking Elizabeth with him and his wife to a tour in Derbyshire, he advances Elizabeth's relationship with Darcy. For, in the course of this tour Elizabeth and her companions visit Pemberley estates. There Elizabeth meets Darcy unexpectedly. This meeting gives Elizabeth an opportunity to know Darcy more intimately and understand his character aright. Mr Gardiner correctly assesses Darcy's love for Elizabeth and tactfully encourages it. Again, it is he who tries to console Jane and Elizabeth after Bingley is taken away from Jane.

Gardiner is practical, active and resourceful. After Lydia's elopement, when all the members of the Bennet family are submerged in the mire of gloom, it is Gardiner who proceeds to London to find out the eloped couple. He is very useful to the Bennets in the present situation. With Darcy's help he arranges for Wickham's marriage with Lydia and it is from his house that Lydia actually goes to the church to be married.

Mr Gardiner is a model of balance, firmness and wisdom. The Bennet family in general and Elizabeth in particular owe much to him. The good breeding and respectability of Mr Gardiner is an invaluable asset to the Bennet family, several of whose members are sadly lacking in those qualities. He is the model of a perfect gentleman and he has been portrayed most admirably by Jane Austen in the novel.

Mrs Bennet

Mrs Bennet is a woman of a silly vulgar type, who can destroy the happiness of her husband on the one side and hamper the ambitions of her daughters on the other. She is a satirical picture of "a woman of mean understanding, little information and uncertain temper." Her folly and vulgarity prove to be a heavy liability for the entire family, depriving her husband of all chances of domestic felicity and damaging the fortunes of her two eldest daughters, Jane and Elizabeth, by publicly exhibiting her stupidity and ill-breeding.

Mrs Bennet is the daughter of an attorney in Meryton, who has left her five thousand pounds. She has a sister married to a Mr Philips who had been a clerk to their father and has succeeded him in his business. She has also a brother, Mr Gardiner, settled in London in a respectable line of trade. Her physical charm has secured a husband for her, but her stupidity has made her forfeit his good opinion and love for ever. She has five daughters and she is always preoccupied with the problems of their marriage. Jane Austen speaks of her: "The business of her life was to get her daughters married; its solace was visiting and news." The moment she hears that the Netherfield Park has been let out, she immediately tells her husband: "My dear Mr Bennet ... have you heard that Netherfield Park is let at last?" And when she gets a negative reply, she desperately tells him referring to the new tenant, Mr Bingley: "My dear Mr Bennet ... how can you be so tiresome! You must know that I am thinking of his marrying one of them."

It is impossible to form a correct estimate of Mrs Bennet without mentioning some of her follies and vulgarities. Her behaviour at supper after the dance at Netherfield is an outstanding instance of her vulgarity. On this occasion she speaks aloud at the table of her pleasure at Jane's rapid conquest of Bingley's heart. Her studied discourtesy for several weeks to the Lucases solely because the eldest Miss Lucas has become engaged to Mr Collins who must have been by right Elizabeth's husband, is another instance of her ill-breeding. The worst instance of her vulgarity is her behaviour on hearing the news of Lydia's elopement and later of her marriage. Not having the sense to understand this scandalous episode in its full significance, she bursts into intemperate joy on hearing of Lydia's marriage and thinks of how to celebrate it gorgeously.

The stupidity of Mrs Bennet is almost as exasperating as her vulgarity. She has no idea of what an entail exactly is, and in her ignorance she can forgive neither husband for not preventing it nor Mr Collins for deriving benefit from it. Not only this; her stupidity stands in the way of her understanding any person rightly. She is unable to see either the fool in Mr Collins or the rogue in Mr Wickham. And as regards Darcy, she considers him the most disagreeable man and credits herself for being able to tolerate him whenever he visits Longbourn in the company of Mr Bingley. But the moment she learns that this rich young man is going to be her prospective son-in-law, all her dislikes for him disappear at once.

Mrs Bennet is unscrupulous in her views and manners. To her the end justifies the means. In her eagerness to see Jane married to Bingley, she plans to send Jane to Netherfield on horseback so that in case it rains she will be completely drenched and fall ill and thus she can be detained by Bingley for a long period during which an attachment may grow between them. She is not worried about her daughter falling ill as a consequence of her planning.

Mrs Bennet is unpolished, clumsy and undignified in her

manners and expressions. The way she behaves and talks with the different people in the society is most awkward and shows her lack of culture. In a social gathering she becomes the butt of everybody's oblique smile and ironical remarks. One of the reasons given by Darcy for detaching Bingley from Jane is the most sluggish and clumsy manners of Mrs Bennet.

Mrs Bennet is extremely selfish, mean and narrow-minded. When she hears of Bingley's hiring the Netherfield Park she wants her husband to be the first among the callers on him, lest some others of her neighbours should catch him for their daughters. When Collins's marriage with Charlotte Lucas is settled, her behaviour towards this innocent girl undergoes a remarkable change as, by marrying Collins, she is going to be the joint owner with Collins of their entailed estate at Longbourn. For days together she is not in speaking terms with her and does not show the common courtesy of congratulating her on her engagement to Collins.

But with all her defects, she is not deprived by the novelist of one good quality. She is a good housewife. In planning dinners, in arranging walks, in sending out her daughters to balls, she is quite efficient. She takes all possible care to see that the dishes are tasteful and well-prepared. She is an anxious mother too. All her excesses are due to her earnest desire to see her daughters married. But all her efforts in this direction instead of facilitating the matter for her daughters makes it more complicated. We do not despise her; we pity her.

Miss Caroline Bingley

Pride and Prejudice presents two pathetic female characters. One is Mrs Bennet eager to see her daughters married and the other is Miss Caroline Bingley desperately trying to win for herself the hand of Darcy, the hero of the novel. If in her absurd attempts to find husbands for her daughters Mrs Bennet is vulgar, in her efforts to lay a snare for Darcy Miss Bingley is detestable and despicable. Yet, by an irony, not infrequent in a civilized society, the despicable woman prides herself on her refinement and looks down with contempt on anybody who is not nearly as despicable as she herself is.

Miss Bingley's only object in life seems to be her acceptance by Darcy as his wife. So she is desperate and mad in her efforts to win Darcy. Her one study is to catch Darcy's attention and win his applause. She feeds him with flattery, praises his sister, his estates, his knowledge, his tastes, in fact, everything down to his ease and quickness of writing. When at Netherfield she fails to attract Darcy's attention, she stops reading a book and starts pacing the room up and down so that Darcy might observe her and be attracted by her graceful presence. But she does not succeed and ultimately asks Elizabeth as to what to do. And Elizabeth sarcastically remarks: "Teaze him — laugh at him" (Chapter 11).

It is a bitter irony that Miss Bingley's unceasing pursuit of Darcy has the inevitable effect of making him despise her. Ignorant of the real effect of her servile adoration of Darcy, she continues to flatter him. But when it does not produce the desired result, she tries to lead her brother into loving Darcy's sister so that his marriage might improve her chances of marrying Darcy. And when this strategy fails and she finds to her mortification that Darcy is becoming attentive to Elizabeth, she commits the fatal folly of calumniating her rival. But this only increases Darcy's dislike for her.

Miss Bingley is shallow, short-sighted and extremely self-centred. The shallowness of her character becomes obvious when, after failing in her attempts to get Darcy as her husband, she thinks that she should not lose the opportunity of visiting Darcy's grand Pemberley House, by conciliating Elizabeth for the favour of being accepted as a friend. She is short-sighted as she fails to realize Darcy's growing affection for Elizabeth, and unwisely starts the policy of criticizing Elizabeth before Darcy. All this further alienates Darcy from her.

The immodesty, insincerity and snobbery of Miss Bingley are intended to serve as admirable foils to the virtues of the two eldest Bennet girls, Jane and Elizabeth. The sweetness and modesty of Jane's disposition become all the more charming when set off against the vulgarity and spitefulness of Miss Bingley. The courage and frankness of Elizabeth become sterling virtues when contrasted with the servility and hypocrisy of Miss Bingley. Thus, Miss Bingley is a disagreeable character. She is a clear example of social pride and class prejudice arising out of her beauty, riches and social rank.

Charlotte Lucas

Charlotte Lucas is the eldest daughter of Sir William Lucas. She is introduced by Jane Austen as "a sensible, intelligent young woman, about twenty-seven ... Elizabeth's intimate friend" (Chapter 5). She is quite conscious about the need of a practical marriage. Security, rather than romance, according to her, should be the basis of marriage. Even in matter of courtship she is quite practical. She objects to the reticence of Jane and tells Elizabeth that unless Jane speaks out her feelings openly to Bingley, she will be misunderstood by him. So, Jane must make some efforts to make Bingley understand her properly. Charlotte herself practises what she preaches. She accepts Collins's proposal in a worldly-wise manner. Elizabeth might feel shocked at her friend's acceptance of Collins's proposal, but Charlotte, who is seven years older than her friend, Elizabeth, knows that the security of a husband with a steady income is more important than love and understanding. This shows her prudent and materialistic outlook on life.

Charlotte is a good friend. So, even after her friend Elizabeth is upset by her marriage with Collins, she pursues the friendship and invites her to Hunsford and thus allows Elizabeth an opportunity to meet Darcy once again, which subsequently paves the way for Elizabeth's self-realization and rapid movement of the story to its culmination.

Charlotte acts as a contrast to Elizabeth in her practical and rational attitude to life. But this contrast is quite natural. Elizabeth is younger than Charlotte and has less experience of life. But Charlotte has seen more of life and has experience of its hardship. She is already past the marriageable age and so to her a home and the security of a husband with a steady income is more important than love and understanding. So she says that it is better to know as little as possible of the defects of the person with whom she is going to pass her life. She agrees with Elizabeth about the unlikeable features of Collins's character. But she has sacrificed her better feeling to worldly advantage. The lesson of Charlotte's marriage teaches Elizabeth, as nothing else can, that practical considerations are both important to, and possible in, a marriage — a realization that is vital before Elizabeth can marry Darcy.

Lady Catherine de Bourgh

Lady Catherine de Bourgh is the sister of Darcy's mother and owner of Rosings estate. She is the most repulsive of the characters who appear in the novel. Collins, with all his absurdity, manages to win our sympathy. Mrs Bennet and Miss Bingley may have some claim to our pity. And despite his levity we can even go to the extent of forgiving Wickham. But for Lady Catherine we have nothing but contempt and dislike and not a bit of sympathy or pity.

It is through Mr Collins that we first come to know of her. During his visit to Longbourn Collins repeatedly refers to the name of Lady Catherine who is his patroness. For him at least she is a lady of exceptionally fine behaviour, generous and merciful and possessing a high rank and noble breeding. Lady Catherine has conferred the parsonage of Hunsford upon Mr Collins and by that act of patronage has earned his life-long gratitude and devotion.

Lady Catherine is a rich dowager, the owner of a vast property in Hunsford. She has an only daughter, an invalid, whom she dreams of giving in marriage to her nephew Darcy, so that the two rich houses of Pemberley and Hunsford may be united. With a dictatorial frame of mind and unaccustomed to face any refusal, she looks forward to this marriage as a certainty.

Lady Catherine is very much fond of flattery. She accepts the blind adoration of Mr Collins as something strictly due to her and she treats him all the while in a spirit of sanctified pride and lofty condescension. Her acceptance of the adoration of Collins appears to us as nothing but ridiculous.

In a sense Lady Catherine may be called an egoist. She regards herself as infallible and always morally upright. She considers herself the sole master of all things. She moves with an air of dignity and thinks that everyone should have the same interest as she has, in her high social position and wealth. Thus, she is self-opinionated and arrogant. She is the dictator and oracle combined in one. No problem is beyond her wisdom and no detail is beneath her curiosity.

Lady Catherine is silly and ever assertive. She every now and then gives uncalled for advice and suggestion. She inspects, superintends and directs the house management of Mr Collins. She is always decisive and never allows her opinions to be discussed and doubted. She is not in the habit of praising anybody for anything good in him or her. Thus as she considers music to be her favourite subject, she shows interest in Elizabeth's playing the pianoforte, but she is not prepared to praise her.

Lady Catherine is stupid and unmannerly. Her stupidity and absurdity are exposed when, on hearing about the rumour of Darcy's engagement to Elizabeth, she rushes to Longbourn to meet Elizabeth. She has the presumption to imagine that Elizabeth would never dare to look so high for marriage and therefore does not believe in the rumour. But, since her own daughter's prospects are at stake, she does not wish to take any chances. So, she has come to Elizabeth to verify the truth of it. She takes it for granted that she has only to warn Elizabeth against the engagement and her object will be gained. In this arrogant expectation she calls on Elizabeth and demands from her an undertaking that she will never be engaged to Darcy. But to her dismay she receives a stern refusal from Elizabeth to give any such undertaking. She is shocked to find that her authority is flouted by a girl belonging to a humble station in life. She goes to Darcy to complain against Elizabeth, which produces the result opposite to the one expected.

Lady Catherine's main purpose in the novel is to throw light on Elizabeth's character, first when Elizabeth stands up to her at Rosings and later at Longbourn where she proves her worth by refusing to concede to the demand of Lady Catherine. Thus, Elizabeth defeats pride and prejudice combined in the character of Lady Catherine. This final act of stupidity of Lady Catherine brings Darcy and Elizabeth together by encouraging Darcy to propose to Elizabeth.

Lydia Bennet

Lydia is the youngest daughter of the Bennets. She is a stout well-grown girl of fifteen with high animal spirits and, according to her father, one of the silliest girls in the country. She is the most forward and independent girl among the Bennet daughters. We actually hear very little about her for the first two-thirds of the novel. We see her as an attractive young girl whose sole interests are clothes, dancing and men. Both she and her sister Catherine are very much fond of visiting their aunt at Meryton where a military regiment has been stationed. She and her sister like to hang around Meryton spotting various handsome officers, dance with them at balls and store up gossip about them. Lydia's fondness for these officers has been the very opposite of real friendship or love. She does not know any of the soldiers as people but falls for the image and appearance of the soldier. She is a flirt and will never care to see how much defamation and ridicule her flirtation will bring to her family. Her only happiness lies in flirting with at least six army officers at once.

It is this attraction for military men that makes Lydia an easy prey for Wickham. The story of her elopement begins when Elizabeth returns to Longbourn from Collins's parsonage. Before that we learn from Darcy's letter about Wickham's unsuccessful attempt at eloping with Darcy's sister. Lydia is a victim of her passions. The idea that she will finally marry a young military officer and thus will be able to satisfy her passions makes her decide at once to go to Brighton, even though Elizabeth advises her not to go. She is vain, ignorant and absolutely uncontrolled. Her ignorance and rashness ultimately results in her eloping with Wickham, as she is unable to foresee the dangerous implications of such an elopement. In Jane Austen's day a girl was unmarriageable if she had eloped, and once her parents were dead, she was possibly without means of support. Lydia falls for Wickham without considering this, let alone the family disgrace. Her sense of fun, her stubbornness and her sheer ignorance of Wickham's real nature and her own actions, all make her an easy victim.

Lydia is shameless and not repentant. When Lydia returns to Longbourn, she has all that her mother has brought her up to want: a handsome husband, a wedding ring and married status. She giggles and patronizes her sisters until she leaves.

She remains still untamed, unabashed, wild, noisy and fearless. She is insensible to the disgrace she has brought on her family by her elopement with Wickham, and when the two fugitives are found out and Wickham, the villain, is compelled to marry Lydia, she is found turning from sister to sister demanding their congratulations. Jane Austen has presented through Lydia one aspect of womanhood in which passing sensation, fun and flirtation, attraction and attention rule the life. In many ways Lydia is the opposite of every other woman in the novel: quiet and restrained Jane, practical and intelligent Charlotte, clever and sophisticated Caroline. Above all, she is the opposite of the heroine Elizabeth whose awareness, intelligence and sensitive approach allow her to gain a good and stable relationship, of which Lydia is deprived. Lydia's marriage to Wickham is characterized by a lack of money, which reflects their growing lack of affection, and her letter to Elizabeth in the last chapter seeking the assistance of Darcy in gaining for Wickham a position at court, shows that she is still as impudent and thoughtless as ever. The failure of Lydia's marriage at the end of the novel is Jane Austen's final condemnation of her and what she represents.

Lydia is not a likeable character, though she may have a great deal of our sympathy. She is self-centred, rude and shows little real kindness to anyone. She is both innocent and ignorant of love and life and she never has the opportunity to learn better. She is condemned to a life with a man who does not love her and we can imagine her, like her mother, a pitiful figure in later life. She plays an important role in the development of the plot, though indirectly, by her elopement which ultimately brings Darcy and Elizabeth close to each other resulting in their marriage, and also helps in the union of Jane and Bingley.

Mary Bennet

Mary Bennet is the third daughter among the five Bennet daughters. She is a voracious reader and is always anxious to show off her erudition by quoting from the books she has read. She is the plainest looking of all the Bennet girls. To make matters worse she has a serious and moralizing way of talking picked up from her studies, which makes her very unimpressive. She is unable to establish normal relations with people around her and so she retreats in her world of books. Jane Austen perhaps wants to burlesque through Mary those people whose knowledge, derived from books, remains unrelated to life. Mary has neither the experience nor the guidance to benefit from the study. She wants to say something sensible but does not know how to do it. Her communications with her family are limited to platitudes, stock responses and moralizing. She seems predestined to end her days as a spinster. Her looks are plain, her temperament is too serious and her habits are too unsociable. When all her sisters left Longbourn permanently, she remains with her mother to take care of her. She is not much connected with the main story of the novel. Yet she is not an unconvincing character. Jane Austen has made her a living and likeable character by her superb art of characterization.

Catherine Bennet (Kitty)

Catherine Bennet is the fourth daughter of Mr and Mrs Bennet. She is only seventeen. She is of delicate health. According to Mr Bennet she is one of the two silliest of his daughters, the other being Lydia. She is sickly and often coughs so hard that her parents complain of it. Mrs Bennet says: "Don't keep coughing so, Kitty, for heaven's sake! Have a little compassion on my nerves. You tear them to pieces." Mr Bennet also remarks as he leaves the room: "Now, Kitty, you may cough as much as you choose." Lydia is her constant companion. Like Lydia, Catherine also is flirtatious. Her life seems to be completely devoted to dancing, gossiping, flirting and dressing. She especially likes men in uniform. This makes her a very good companion of Lydia. She knows all about Lydia's intended elopement but never reveals it. This shows her genuine affection for her sister. After Jane and Elizabeth are married, she lives with one or other of them. She then becomes less irritable, less ignorant and less insipid under the improving influence of her sisters Jane and Elizabeth.

13

Jane Austen's Moralistic Outlook

Although not exactly didactic, Jane Austen's novels betray at least a moralistic outlook. Names of her novels like *Sense and Sensibility, Pride and Prejudice* suggest a kind of sermonization to the readers. In *Pride and Prejudice* Elizabeth is shown as the embodiment of prejudice and Darcy, as the embodiment of pride. The conflict between them, leading to an ultimate reconciliation and union in marriage, is the theme of the novel. As a moralist, concerned with the principles of right and wrong, she reveals the wrongness of human behaviour and either reforms the character or shows the sufferings as a consequence of the wrong behaviour. In this respect she appears to have been greatly influenced by Dr Johnson. Like Johnson she refuses to express a deeper concern than what she feels for misfortune or grief. Her morality is not merely embodied in her plots. It is openly expressed through the characters and their actions. Her statements and comments on various situations and characters are often well worth serious examination.

Jane Austen is a moralist, but somewhat different from the conventional type. She expresses her dislike for some wrong actions or behaviour, but does not openly condemn them. She allows full play to emotion or imagination, however disagreeable or prosaic it may be. It is her sense of humour that keeps her from being harsh to the stupid characters, as other novelists like Fielding and Smollett were. She is never angry with her characters. She has only contempt for the silly, the affected and the stupid characters. She is neither an interpreter nor a critic of life. She is merely its keen and sensitive observer. She is satisfied and contented to play the role of an observer, observing the multifarious activities of life. Like a true moralist she has little romanticism in her. She is rather serious. The romantic guidance of all the instinctive movements of heart and imagination is profoundly alien to her. To her, emotions have but little value. In *Pride and Prejudice* we find that even love gets its justification when it is governed by reason and disciplined by self-control. Thus, the love of Lydia and Wickham does not get her approval. To her life is a game of matrimony in which reason is predominant over everything else. She has shown the folly of trusting the first impressions in Elizabeth's treatment of Darcy and Wickham, and it is Elizabeth's mature observation and realization of her folly that finally resolve all the complications.

It is her eighteenth century background that makes Jane Austen profoundly moral in her outlook. She thinks that wc live only to be good and that it is the primary duty of everyone to be sincere, unselfish, honest and disinterested. But she is not an idealist. She does not value ideals however lofty they may be, if they are not practical. She despises all emotions, however, soul-stirring, if they do not, in fact, make for the benefit or happiness of mankind. Thus, in a sense, she is a realist. And this realism makes her think that life is at best an imperfect affair and it is not wise to worry about evils which cannot be prevented. Hence, life has to be lived and should be lived. This robust and realistic attitude lies at the basis of Jane Austen as a moralist.

Jane Austen does not preach any moral. She is not a deliberate preacher using her literary creations as her mouthpieces. She is after truth and nothing less than truth and so there is no sense in preaching and talking about it. For, to all sensible persons it will be obvious. Jane Austen's moral outlook is tempered by her mature common sense and her ability to separate the basis of a problem from other unimportant matters. As a novelist her main concern is with the development of well-knit plots and articulate characters moving in the midst of interesting situations. But since her art is so deeply realistic and tempered by her innate sensibilities, she cannot avoid expressing her moral attitude which is rational and practical and which adds considerably to the verisimilitude and sobriety of her artistic creations.

Jane Austen has her own standard of moral judgment. This standard is evolved out of her characteristic self-command, just consideration for others, knowledge of the heart and a principle of rightness derived from education. In her world all the errors and follies of the youth are almost always the result of a faulty upbringing. Thus, she considers society and not the individual so much responsible for the wrong-doings. That is why she thinks that behind the wickedness of Lydia in her elopement with Wickham lies the foolishness of her mother and the indifference and irresponsibility of her father. She traces the consequences of the follies in her characters in her world of fiction. In the real world the consequences may be otherwise. But in her world of imagination the fools and the knaves are not spared. Yet, she does not have any theory of art or any philosophy of life. In her novels she holds up the mirror to her times. She realizes that life is a mixture of good and bad. She thinks that out of it one can draw a great deal of fun. She does not approve of the follies and misdeeds. But passing them by with a look of disapproval she remains contented to look at the panorama of life and creates a world of amusement and delight for her readers.

14

Jane Austen's Style

Jane Austen herself once described her own style perfectly as "a little bit of ivory, two inches wide on which I work with a brush so fine as to produce little effect after much labour." Her style is a model of clarity and purity. When she chooses an expression she takes care to see that it is precise and in balance with everything else. With the lucidity and clarity of expression she makes it a point to remain objective, and if she at all expresses her attitude she does it indirectly. The main qualities of her style of narration are precision, economy and directness. In the technical excellence she is unsurpassed. In the construction of plot, in the development of characters and in the artistic display of dramatic situations, she may be ranked among the great masters of the art. Bradley says of her: "Nobody ever opened a novel or managed an exposition better than Jane Austen who would deserve immortality if she had written only the first chapter of *Pride and Prejudice.*" Few English novelists possess the knowledge of the art of writing fiction to perfection. Scott allows slip-shod work to creep into his novels. Dickens is notoriously careless in construction. Even Thackeray does not come up to the perfection of Jane Austen's art. An all pervasive point of view, easily appreciated by the common reader, constitutes Jane Austen's singular charm. This point of view is humorous in the best sense of the term, looking at the manifold follies of life with a kindly tolerant smile.

Irony is the hallmark of Jane Austen's style. Dramatic irony is used quite frequently by Jane Austen, particularly in *Pride and Prejudice*. This is to be found in Mrs Bennet's artless exclamation: "My dear Mr Bennet you must not expect such girls to have the sense of their father and mother." Mr Collins's proposal to Elizabeth similarly displays his pompous idiocy. He gives the reasons to Elizabeth for his decision to marry her. He says that he is "convinced it will add very greatly to my happiness." Besides, his patroness, Lady Catherine, has told him: "Mr Collins you must marry. A clergyman like you must marry." Again, Mr Bennet is always witty and ironical in his speech. Of course, he is often cynical and sneering. He is also irresponsible in his wit sometimes. Jane Austen's use of irony is a means of exposing truth with subtlety and economy. The description of Miss Bingley and Mrs Hurst, the two sisters, from the point of view of Elizabeth in chapter 4 shows remarkable economy and clarity. Again, it is ironical, too, and stimulating and amusing in itself. They are called "very fine ladies," yet all the unpleasant qualities like pride and conceit, snobbery and selfishness are attributed to them. This kind of pleasant irony is to be found everywhere in the novel.

Jane Austen does not use similes or metaphors, but the use of antithesis, anticlimax and irony is not infrequent in her novels. The discreet use of these ornamentations makes her narrative highly delightful. Jane Austen can also sustain the reader's interest in her long-drawn description or narration by her attention to minute details and her breathless speed of narration. She, however, does not have anything of the pompous or verbose about her prose which is disciplined, quiet and simple. The precision and economy of her expression may be found in her observations on Mrs Bennet's character at the end of chapter 1. There she writes: "She was a woman of mean understanding, little information, and uncertain temper. When she was discontented she fancied herself nervous. The business of her life was to get her daughters married; its solace was visiting and news." This is a nice summing up of Mrs Bennet's character as has already been demonstrated in the chapter by her conversation with her husband. There is irony in her observations on Mrs Bennet's character, as also on the characters of Miss Bingley and Mrs Hurst.

Jane Austen's novel is imbued with a dramatic quality. Quite naturally dialogues play a very important part and the dialogues are introduced by means of a device in which the novelist expounds a character's views in terms obviously appropriate to his or her way of thinking, but keeps to the sequence of tenses belonging to indirect speech. The wording and the intonation belong to direct speech, but the grammatical structure, to indirect speech. This style admirably helps Jane Austen to magnify the ludicrousness of human pride and presumption and introduce a subtle but restrained undercurrent of irony. Jane Austen has a remarkable ear and she is a shrewd observer of the peculiarities in speech. So, the speeches of her characters are always consistent with their personalities. Thus Collins's speeches are full of cliché and pomposity. Mr Bennet's speeches are witty and satirical. Mrs Bennet's speeches are foolish and extravagant. A similar skill is displayed by Jane Austen in the letters which the different characters write. Thus Collins's letter to Mr Bennet is full of pomposity and studied formality while Lydia's letter to Mrs Forster reveals clearly her feather-headed hectic silliness. Jane Austen has written her novel mostly in the form of dialogues and the dialogues have been so artfully framed as not merely to reveal character but also to develop the action and point to the themes of the novel.

15

Significance of the Opening Chapter of *Pride and Prejudice*

The first chapter of any book is of great importance. It introduces us to the main themes and characters and involve us in what is going to happen. The opening chapter of *Pride and Prejudice* is also significant for the same reason. It starts with a general statement: "It is a truth universally acknowledged that a single man in possession of a good fortune must be in want of a wife." This statement is ironical which will be revealed in course of the novel. It also hints at the main theme of the novel. The novel deals with the business of marriage. And the novel starts by presenting before us a family with five unmarried daughters with their mother anxious to get them married. So, the moment she hears that a rich young bachelor has settled in their neighbourhood, she becomes eager to catch him for one of her daughters. In this way the opening chapter also gives us an indication of the future events. We remain in eager expectation to know whether Mrs Bennet will be able to get the young bachelor, Mr Bingley, as the husband of one of her daughters.

The opening chapter also introduces to the readers the important characters of the novel. The first chapter of *Pride and Prejudice* reveals to us the important traits of the characters of Mr and Mrs Bennet and their attitude towards their daughters. Mr Bennet has tender feelings towards Elizabeth, his second daughter, who is most sensible and far-sighted among all the Bennet daughters. Jane, the eldest of the Bennet girls, is, however, the favourite of her mother, Mrs Bennet. We also learn that Jane is more beautiful and elegant than Elizabeth.

Jane Austen has given a graphic portraiture of Mr Bennet and Mrs Bennet through their conversation and crowns it at the end of the chapter by commenting on these two characters. She says that Mr Bennet was an admixture of quick parts, sarcastic humour, reserve and caprice, and Mrs Bennet was a woman of mean understanding, little information and uncertain temper. The future events in the novel go to prove the truth of these remarks about the two characters. Mr Bennet is really a man of sarcastic humour, reserved and indifferent towards the day-to-day happenings of life. Mrs Bennet reveals her foolishness, ignorance and vulgarity by her words and behaviour.

The opening chapter also reveals the wonderful craftsmanship of Jane Austen. It has been well said that Jane Austen was the first novelist to give the world really alive novels. Her ability to blend realism with artistic patterns results in the creation of a world which is vibrant and pulsating. The opening chapter of *Pride and Prejudice* gives us a glimpse of this ability of the novelist. "In the wonderful first chapter of *Pride and Prejudice* which comes alive so immediately and gives so sharp and yet so subtle a sense of life; so that we know at once so much about the Bennet family, this 'life' would not be there but for Jane Austen's tone, her ironical opening generalization, her choice of words, her italics, her decision at each point and moment as to just how and where her reader's attention shall be directed" (Arnold Kettle). The opening chapter of *Pride and Prejudice*, thus, illustrates the unique artistic quality of Jane Austen, the superb craftsman.

16

The Narrow World of Jane Austen

Jane Austen deliberately keeps herself away from all sensational and interesting material however historically important or of contemporary significance, and concentrates her attention upon the thoughts, feelings, motives and prejudices of common men and women. The world she places her characters in, is limited to the one she is acquainted with. She writes to her niece: "Three or four families in a country village is the very thing to work upon." Her small world is that of the provincial gentry. She is not concerned with the rustic people or the agricultural labourers who must have been numerous around Longbourn and Meryton. The industrial masses of big cities also are beyond her purview. Even the important political affairs that disturb the city life and the life of men in general do not have any effect on the life presented in her novel. The world of *Pride and Prejudice* is a world of balls, dinners, visits, walks, tours and talks about marriages. And the characters that people the novel belong to the upper middle-class. Jane Austen consciously omits the lower classes, the servants, and the aristocracy. And when she presents any member of the aristocracy, it is only to satirize them. Lady Catherine de Bourgh is the daughter of an earl, but instead of presenting her as a dignified and respectable character, she is made to appear as an arrogant, pretentious and stupid woman who can only rouse the reader's disdain. Colonel Fitzwilliam is a flat and functional character existing only perhaps to buttress Elizabeth's prejudice by telling her how Darcy has been instrumental in breaking up the attachment between Bingley and Jane.

The movements of the characters of *Pride and Prejudice* are mostly limited to the countryside. The world of Jane Austen is limited to Longbourn, Netherfield, Meryton, Hunsford and Pemberley. This is particularly because Jane Austen herself was a country girl and remained a country girl all through. And while writing she never wants to go beyond her own personal experience. No discerning reader will ever fail to notice the restraint she has voluntarily imposed on herself. Her world is limited geographically, socially and even morally. We do not find the extremes of love, hate, evil and even righteousness in her novel. Jane Austen never uses her characters as vehicles for ethical or metaphysical tenets. She is content to present her little world as truthfully as she can.

As the novel is based on Jane Austen's personal experience, the characters appear to us as the most living, authentic human beings. We seem to know the characters intimately. We enter into their world unawares and share their feelings of joy and sorrow. Thus, Jane Austen's world may be narrow, but out of it she can develop themes of the broadest significance. It is her moral complexity that brightens her themes. Her world may be limited, but within the limits she has set for herself, she reigns supreme. Genius may be as well employed in telling the story of a village as in dealing with the fall of an empire. But in either case the product of a genius must be superb. And Jane Austen has done the same in *Pride and Prejudice* by telling us a quiet domestic tale. It is her great artistic gift and pure technical excellence that have raised the novel to its high pedestal, although it does not encompass a wide world with its varied movements and complexities.

17

A Summing-up

F.R. Leavis in his book *The Great Tradition* has observed that Jane Austen inaugurated the great tradition of fiction and he considers her the first novelist of England. But in studying her as a novelist we should consider her in the context of the eighteenth century. Of course, she has more of Addison, Goldsmith and Fanny Burney than of Fielding, Sterne or Mrs Radcliffe. It is not an easy task to locate her place in the history of fiction. We cannot call her a Romantic in spite of her closeness to Wordsworth and Coleridge. At the same time we cannot call her a classical writer because of her great proximity to her age.

Jane Austen is a realist. She has given to the novel an art and style which we find in Fielding. Fielding was the master of two styles, the burlesque and the rich eloquence of the great orators and moralists. Jane Austen has revived something of this style to which she has added an element of beauty and attractiveness by using the language of everyday life. In the delineation of characters and handling of events she leaves much less to chance than did Fielding. Jane Austen brings together her village folk and their visitors at the dinner party and the ball as naturally as they meet in real life. But it will be wrong to infer that she merely transcribes actual experiences. She builds up scenes in her imagination taking details from her various experiences and creates a comedy of manners which is distinct from real life. *Pride and Prejudice* gives a detailed picture of country life in walks, dances, parties and gossips, yet it cannot be called a faithful record of contemporary life. It is rather a successful attempt at studying human behaviour. Macaulay appreciates it and says that Jane Austen has given us a multitude of characters, all in a certain sense commonplace, yet they are all as perfectly discriminated from each other as if they are the most eccentric of human beings.

Pride and Prejudice may be said to be a grand specimen of a miniature painting. The entire plot of the novel is knit round the institution of family which is a world of its own where one will fail to find any sensational incident. The men and women in the novel are quite ordinary persons whom we often meet in our everyday life. And they fill the world of *Pride and Prejudice* and make it appear as a piece of wonderful painting. The novel has also been compared to an opera of Mozart by Brower in his article, "Jane Austen's controlling hand." In an opera the words form one entity, and the orchestration, another, and these two, the recital and the symphony, make a whole. In Mozart the symphony offers a commentary on the recital. In the same way the characters in Jane Austen's novel speak freely but their actions and interactions upon each other produce a commentary. This technique of an opera has been successfully employed by Jane Austen in *Pride and Prejudice*.

Jane Austen in her narration is but ostensibly objective. Sometimes she poses as a historian possessing all the facts narrating them dispassionately. Sometimes again she seems to record facts as she finds them happening. Yet she does not allow the facts to speak for themselves. She often intrudes to give her own comments on the situation and characters.

Jane Austen takes a comic view of the world. The follies and foibles, illusions and self-contradictions of human nature are a joy to her for their own sake and also because through action they lead to consequences which may be serious, but may also be comic. The errors, misunderstandings and cross-purposes which these defects in human nature create, produce sometimes matter fit for comedy. This point of view not merely of humour but of comedy as well is so marked in Jane Austen's novel as to suggest the influence of drama on her. There are not a few dialogues in her novel, which might be transferred, with scarcely any change, to the stage. Some scenes which are open to criticism as parts of a novel, are quite suitable for a drama.

For example, Mr Collins's proposal to Elizabeth, delightful as it is, suggests nothing but farce. Again, Mary, the third of the Bennet sisters, appears always in the same attitude like a stock figure in a comedy. And Mr Bennet seems almost to be made for the drama.

There is a strain of morality in Jane Austen's attitude to situations and characters in her novel. This is noticed in her marked distrust of any indulgence in emotion or imagination where these are not plainly subservient to the resolve to do the right thing. She has hatred of all ideals, however lofty, which are not practical, and of all emotions, however soul-stirring, if they do not make for the benefit and happiness of mankind. Love itself does not rouse her enthusiasm unless it is justified by reason and disciplined by self-control. She has little sympathy for romantic imprudence or credulous good nature. She believes that it is wrong to marry for money, but at the same time she is of the opinion that it is silly to marry without it. Her moralistic outlook has made her satirical, but she is not bitter. This is because of her acceptance of life with all its goodness and evil. She does not certainly approve of the wickedness and stupidity of the people. But she is amused by such characters and treats them ironically. Irony is the soul of Jane Austen's comedy.

Jane Austen is not flawless in presenting her characters. Darcy exists mostly to play in scenes with Elizabeth. He may appear real and convincing, but we do not know quite enough about him. Again, his extreme insolence at the first ball does not quite match his later behaviour. Even in delineating minor characters Miss Austen shows some lack of skill. Mary is carelessly done. She is not even very funny. Kitty is a little better managed. Mr Collins and Lady Catherine, however, appear greatly entertaining.

Jane Austen's presentation of the universal human nature makes her the most modern. She is compared to Shakespeare. When we say that Shakespeare is of all time we mean that human nature is of all time and that Shakespeare has told the truth about it. A great tribute to Jane Austen is paid by Walter Allen in his book, *The English Novel*: "Today lady novelists of some wit and concision, who concern themselves with those aspects of upper-class life which can be viewed from the tea-table, are almost invariably compared by reviewers to Jane Austen. It is very rare indeed that they have anything in common with her tough eighteenth-century mind, her severity of values, her miraculous sense of form. Her influence is, rather, diffused and indirect; she has become one of the permanent points of reference by which the achievements of other novelists are measured."

18

Critical Reception of the Novel

Jane Austen was not very popular during her lifetime and she had an extremely hard time finding publishers for her novels. She began writing her first novel, *Pride and Prejudice* sometime in 1797 and completed it by November, the same year, under the title, *First Impressions*. Her father Reverend George Austen, having been impressed by the book, at once sent the manuscript to a London publisher, Cadell. But the publisher declined the offer of buying the copyright of the book, by return of post. Such was the first reception of the novel which was to be acclaimed later as one of the masterpieces of English literature. Sixteen years later, in 1813, the book, in a revised form and under a new title, *Pride and Prejudice*, was offered to a publisher who accepted it and the book was published the very same year. But, even after its publication it did not have much favourable reception at the hands of the contemporary men of letters.

Sir Walter Scott spoke of Jane Austen's tact in characterization and her precision in presenting the subject, yet he observed in "The Quarterly Review" that her "subjects are not often elegant and certainly never grand." He also seemed to misunderstand the story of the novel as he thought that Elizabeth's decision to marry Darcy stemmed largely from her delight in the elegance of Pemberley. Wordsworth acknowledged the accuracy of Austen's delineation of characters, but he did not find any interest in her novel as he did not find in it the truth of nature clarified by the pervading light of imagination. Charlotte Brontë also did not have a favourable opinion. According to her Jane Austen delineated the surface of the lives of the genteel English people with a Chinese fidelity and a miniature delicacy in the painting, but the passions of the human heart were perfectly unknown to her as she was not half so much with the human heart as with the human eyes, hands and feet. But what Charlotte Brontë did not understand was that in Jane Austen's novel passion was there by implication and it was to be guided properly by prudence. Lydia and Wickham were lovers, no doubt, but their love was not under prudent control. Hence Jane Austen made fun of them. Edward FitzGerald complained that Jane Austen never went out of the parlour. This was perhaps because he had never cared to read Elizabeth Bennet's remark to her sister Jane: "The more I see of the world, the more am I dissatisfied with it; and every day confirms my belief of the inconsistency of all human characters, and of the little dependence that can be placed on the appearance of either merit or sense" (Chapter 24). H.W. Garrod made a similar complaint when he observed that Miss Austen's materials comprised a drab scenery the worst for use, a thin plot unfashionably cut and, by turning, relining and trimming made to do the duty for five or six novels and a dozen or so stock characters.

Jane Austen's fame was to come with the later Victorian novelists. And when in the twentieth century the Victorians went out of fashion, Jane Austen became more favourite in England. Among the modern writers Jane Austen found her devotees in Katherine Mansfield and Virginia Woolf. But it is in E.M. Forster that she found one of her greatest admirers. His discussions on Jane Austen in *Aspects of the Novel* (1927) are of great critical interest. He particularly praises Jane Austen's art of characterization. A.C. Bradley's essay on Jane Austen (Jane Austen: A Lecture, 1911) seemed to be the first comprehensive critical work on Jane Austen. Bradley particularly drew the readers' attention to the relationship between Jane Austen's irony and her narrative point of view. R.W. Chapman's edition of the six novels of Jane Austen appeared in 1923. This was followed by his edition of the letters of Jane Austen (1932) and his edition of her earlier and unfinished works (1932). Edwin Muir, another admirer of Jane Austen, spoke of her in his book, *The Structure of the Novel* (1928), that she was "the first novelist who practised it [the dramatic novel] with consummate success in England." And in support of his contention he discussed in detail the plot of *Pride and Prejudice*.

During the thirties and the forties of the twentieth century widespread influence of Freud and Marx led critics to see Jane Austen from new perspectives. Critics now began to find in the four novels of Austen — *Sense and Sensibility, Pride and Prejudice, Mansfield Park* and *Emma* — a reversal of the Oedipus complex. In these novels the female protagonist hated her mother, loved her father, rejected a worthless suitor and finally accepted a dependable lover who appeared to be a father-substitute for her. This comment is a reflection on the character of Elizabeth Bennet in *Pride and Prejudice*. Again, Jane Austen was considered a Marxist before Marx, as she exposed the economic basis of social behaviour with an ironic smile. This is particularly true about the social behaviour of Miss Bingley and Lady Catherine. In the late forties Mark Schorer in his essay "Fiction and the Matrix of Analogy" in *The Kenyan Review* (1949) translated the economic approach to Jane Austen into terms of literary criticism. During the fifties and after, critical and scholarly work on Jane Austen was done more in America than in England. And with the passing of time, Jane Austen's popularity has been increasing, which will be evident from the remark made by Walter Allen in *The English Novel* (1954) that, "Miss Austen was a highly sophisticated artist."

In the twentieth century Jane Austen was looked upon more favourably than she was in the nineteenth. But she did not receive unqualified praise from some of the critics. Thus, David Daiches observed that Miss Austen knew only too well that in the kind of society she portrayed, genteel young ladies could not afford true love and their objective must have been marriage and marriage with someone eligible, who could give her financial security. Against this opinion R.W. Chapman reminded us of Elizabeth's repudiation of Collins, which she did to uphold her love. David Daiches, however, held that, "structurally, the novel shows the highest degree of craftsmanship," and that, "the speed and skill with which the author moves into the story are remarkable." He also had his unstinted praise of the novel as he wrote: "The precision and vivacity of style carry the reader through the novel with ease and spirit; there is a sparkling life about the characters and a rainwashed freshness about the scenery which combine to make this the gayest of Jane Austen's novels." Elizabeth Bowen regarded Jane Austen as having a rigid and conventional sense of values. G.B. Stern and Sheila Kaye-Smith, two women novelists of the period, collaborated in *Talking of Jane Austen* (1943), to pay homage to Miss Austen. Miss Kaye-Smith took into account the costume and the food of the period and the social position of clergymen and also some important political events that took place during Miss Austen's lifetime. Miss Stern was more preoccupied with characters treating them as actual people and classifying them on principles of her own. But both of them agreed that *Pride and Prejudice* did not deserve the topmost place in the list of Jane Austen's novels. Reuben Arthur Brower spoke of *Pride and Prejudice* as sheer poetry of wit. He observed that there are passages in *Pride and Prejudice* in which the rhythmical pattern of the sentence approaches the formal balance of the heroic couplet. According to him Jane Austen combined in this novel the traditions of poetic satire with those of sentimental novel. The union of wit and drama was achieved with complete success in the central sequence of *Pride and Prejudice* in the presentation of Elizabeth and Darcy's gradual revaluation of each other.

Katherine Mansfield and Virginia Woolf were highly appreciative of Jane Austen. Virginia Woolf said of Jane Austen that she was "a mistress of much deeper emotion than appears on the surface." But, it was in E.M. Forster that Jane Austen found one of her most unqualified admirers. Forster spoke highly of the characters of Jane Austen. He wrote: "All the Jane Austen characters are ready for an extended life, for a life which the scheme of her book seldom requires them to lead, and that is why they lead their actual lives so satisfactorily." This is true of all the novels of Jane Austen and particularly of *Pride and Prejudice*. Indeed, Jane Austen is to be remembered for the superb delineation of her characters in her first and best novel,

Pride and Prejudice. Walter Allen has, therefore, rightly observed: "The most popular of her novels has always been *Pride and Prejudice*, because of the brilliant creation of Elizabeth Bennet, a heroine as witty as she is charming." He also remarked: "... what gives her characters their value, what in the deepest sense 'makes' them, is that it is through them that their author expresses a discriminated view of life, a highly serious criticism of life expressed in terms of comedy." It is in the subtle exploration of the deeper recesses of the human psyche and an artistic presentation of those rather than the depiction of the various political and social upheavals, that the real excellence of Jane Austen lies.

Some Important Questions

1. Consider the significance of the title of the novel, *Pride and Prejudice*. Do you think the title a fitting one for the novel?
2. Discuss the appropriateness of the terms 'Pride' and 'Prejudice' used in naming the novel of Jane Austen.
3. *Pride and Prejudice* is a belated specimen of the eighteenth century novel of manners. Is it an adequate description of the novel? Give reasons for your answer.
4. Jane Austen's special contribution to the novel is her presentation of social life with irony and realism. Discuss with reference to *Pride and Prejudice*.
5. *Pride and Prejudice* gives a satisfying picture of eighteenth century English society. — Discuss.
6. Is it justifiable to consider *Pride and Prejudice* as only a charming comedy of manners or is there a more serious intention that can be considered moral? Give reasons for your answer.
7. Money and marriage are the major themes in *Pride and Prejudice*. Show how Jane Austen handles these themes in her novel.
8. Should Jane Austen be regarded as a serious novelist? Answer with reference to *Pride and Prejudice*.
9. Discuss Jane Austen's treatment of 'prudential' motive in marriage with reference to *Pride and Prejudice*.
10. Does the theme of marriage in *Pride and Prejudice* reveal any serious pattern? Give reasons for your answer.
11. Discuss Jane Austen's use of irony for moral and comic purposes in *Pride and Prejudice*.

12. Write a note on Jane Austen's mixture of irony and humour in *Pride and Prejudice.*
13. Examine the structure of the novel, *Pride and Prejudice.*
14. "The plot of *Pride and Prejudice* is too neat to be plausible." — Do you agree? Give reasons for your answer.
15. Write a note on the dramatic nature of the plot of *Pride and Prejudice.*
16. "To say that Darcy is proud and Elizabeth, prejudiced is to tell but half the story" (A.H. Wright). — Discuss.
17. Critically examine Jane Austen's narrative technique in *Pride and Prejudice.*
18. Comment on Jane Austen's powers and limitations as a delineator of characters in *Pride and Prejudice.*
19. "Jane Austen's women are more intelligent and life-like than her men." Examine the truth of this remark with special reference to *Pride and Prejudice.*
20. Examine Jane Austen's treatment of comic characters in *Pride and Prejudice.*
21. Discuss Jane Austen's treatment of minor characters in *Pride and Prejudice* with reference to any three of such characters.
22. "*Pride and Prejudice* lives and moves in the character of Elizabeth Bennet." Do you agree? Give reasons for your answer.
23. How far would you accept the view that Darcy is at first a dressed-up idiosyncrasy and then, as the story progresses, he becomes a human being?
24. Comment on the role of Wickham in the development of Elizabeth-Darcy relationship in *Pride and Prejudice.*
25. In *Pride and Prejudice* Jane Austen deals with human incongruities rather than with moral ugliness. — Discuss.
26. Jane Austen did not seek to instruct her readers; her aim was to draw a picture that amuses them. Comment on this remark with suitable illustrations from *Pride and Prejudice.*

27. Jane Austen does not seek to interpret life; she is content to observe it. — Discuss.
28. Comment critically on Jane Austen's style in *Pride and Prejudice*.
29. Describe the ball at Meryton Assembly and show how it is the starting point of the complexities of the plot of *Pride and Prejudice*.
30. Give an account of Elizabeth's visit to Pemberley in the company of Mr and Mrs Gardiner. Show how this visit affects her feelings towards Mr Darcy.
31. By referring closely to the incidents in the novel, explain why the reader finds Mr Collins so objectionable.
32. By reference to the ball scene, where Darcy and Elizabeth first meet, and Darcy's proposal to Elizabeth at Rosings, show how far they reveal Darcy as 'all pride' and Elizabeth as 'all prejudice.'
33. Trace the course of Jane and Bingley's love, paying particular attention to the ways in which their trials and fortunes reveal their characters.
34. How did Darcy give offence in the early part of the novel? What evidence does the novel give of a different, more pleasing Darcy?
35. Give an account of Lady Catherine de Bourgh's visit to Elizabeth at Longbourn, and show how the outcome was very different from what she intended.
36. Bring out the role played by the Gardiners in *Pride and Prejudice*.
37. Describe briefly the episode of elopement of Lydia and Wickham. How does it help in rounding off the story of *Pride and Prejudice*?
38. What is the relevance of the introduction of Georgiana in the novel?
39. Bingley stands as a foil to Darcy in *Pride and Prejudice*. — Discuss.
40. Beside Elizabeth, Jane appears almost as a shadowy figure. — Discuss.

A Select Bibliography

Collected Works and Letters

Austen, Jane. *Novels*. Six volumes. World's Classics. OUP, 1907-31.

The Novels of Jane Austen. Five volumes. Ed. R.W. Chapman. London: OUP, 1923.

Austen, Jane. *Novels*. Six volumes. London: J.M. Dent & Sons Ltd., 1950.

Austen, Jane. *Novels*. Five volumes. Collins Classics. 1953-4.

The Works of Jane Austen. London: Spring Books, 1967.

Austen, Jane. *Selected Letters, 1796-1817*. Ed. R.W. Chapman. OUP, 1955.

Critical and Other Relevant Works

Allen, Walter. *The English Novel*. 1954; rpt. Penguin Books, 1958.

Austen-Leigh, J.S. *A Memoir of Jane Austen*. Ed. R.W. Chapman. Oxford: Clarendon Press, 1926. Reissued 1951.

Baker, E.A. *The History of the English Novel*. Ten volumes. Witherby, 1924-39. (Jane Austen in Volume six).

Bowen, Elizabeth. *Jane Austen*. London, 1936.

Bradley, A.C. "Jane Austen: A Lecture" in The English Association's *Essays and Studies*, Vol. II. Oxford, 1911. (Reprinted in *A Miscellany*. London: Macmillan, 1929).

Brower, R.A. "The Controlling Hand: Jane Austen and *Pride and Prejudice*." *Scrutiny*, No. 13, 1945.

Bush, Douglas. *Jane Austen*. London: Macmillan, 1978.

Cecil, David. *Jane Austen*. Cambridge, 1935.

——. *A Portrait of Jane Austen*. London: Constable, 1978.

——. *Poets and Story-Tellers: A Book of Critical Essays*. London: Constable, 1949.

Chapman, R.W. *Jane Austen: Facts and Problems*. Oxford: Clarendon Press, 1948.

Cox, Constrance. *Pride and Prejudice*. J. Garnet Miller, 1972.

Craik, W.A. *Jane Austen: The Six Novels*. London: Methuen & Co. Ltd., 1965.

Daiches, David. *A Critical History of English Literature*. Vol. III. London: Martin Secker & Warburg Ltd., 1960. Indian Reprint, Allied Publishers Pvt. Ltd., 1979.

Fergus, Jan. *Jane Austen and the Didactic Novel*. London: Macmillan, 1983.

Firkins, O.W. *Jane Austen*. New York, 1920.

FitzGerald, P.H. *Jane Austen: A Criticism and an Appreciation*. London, 1912.

Garrod, H.W. "Jane Austen: A Depreciation" in *Essays by Divers Hands*. London, 1928.

Gillie, C. *A Preface to Jane Austen*. London: Longmans, rev. ed. 1985.

Halliday, E.M. "Narrative Perspective in *Pride and Prejudice*." *Nineteenth Century Fiction*, No. 15. 1961.

Halperin, J. Ed. *Jane Austen: Bicentenary Essays*. Cambridge, 1975.

Harding, D.W. "Regulated Hatred: An Aspect of the Work of Jane Austen." *Scrutiny*, No. 8, 1940.

——. "Jane Austen and Moral Judgment." *Pelican Guide to English Literature*. Vol. V (From Blake to Byron). Harmondsworth, 1957.

Hardwick, Michael. *The Osprey Guide to Jane Austen*. Osprey Publishing, 1973.

Hardy, Barbara. *A Reading of Jane Austen*. London: Athlone Press, 1979.

Jenkins, Elizabeth. *Jane Austen*. London: Victor Gollancz, 1968.

Kennedy, M. *Jane Austen*. 1950. rev. ed. London: Arthur Barker, 1957.

Kliger, S. "Jane Austen's *Pride and Prejudice* in the Eighteenth Century Mode." *University of Toronto Quarterly*. No.16. 1947.

Lascelles, Mary, *Jane Austen and Her Art*. Oxford: Clarendon Press, 1939, Paperback, London: OUP, 1963.

Laski, M. *Jane Austen and Her World*. London: Thames and Hudson, 1969; rpt. 1986.

Lewes, G.H. "The Novels of Jane Austen." *Blackwood's Magazine*. July 1859.

Liddell, Robert, *The Novels of Jane Austen*. London: Allen Lane, 1963.

Litz, A.W. *Jane Austen: A Study of Her Artistic Development*. London: Chatto & Windus, 1965.

Llewelyn, M. *Jane Austen: A Character Study*. William Kimber, 1977.

Mansell, Darrel. *The Novels of Jane Austen: An Interpretation*. London: Macmillan, 1973.

McCann, C.J. "Setting and Character in *Pride and Prejudice*." *Nineteenth Century Fiction*, No, 19. 1965.

Monaghan, David. *Jane Austen in a Social Context*. London: Macmillan, 1981.

Mudrick, M. *Jane Austen: Irony As Defense and Discovery*. Princeton: Princeton University Press, 1952.

Muir, Edwin. *The Structure of the Novel*. London: The Hogarth Press Ltd., 1928. Indian Edition, Allied Publishers Pvt. Ltd., 1966.

Paris, B.J. *Character and Conflict in Jane Austen's Novels*. London, 1979.

Phelps, W.L. *Introduction to Jane Austen's Novels*. London, 1906.

Pinion, F.B. *A Jane Austen Companion: A Critical Survey and Reference Book*. London: Macmillan, 1973.

Sackville, M. *Jane Austen*. London, 1912.

Schorer, M. "Pride Unprejudiced." *Kenyan Review*, No. 18. 1956.

Sherry, Norman. *Jane Austen*. London: Evans Bros., 1966.

Simon, I. "Jane Austen and the Art of the Novel" *English Studies*, No. 43, 1962.

Southam, B.C. *Jane Austen: Sense and Sensibility, Pride and Prejudice and Mansfield Park*. A Casebook. London: Macmillan, 1976.

——. *Jane Austen: The Critical Heritage*. New Delhi: Vikas Publishing House, 1968.

——. Ed. *Critical Essays on Jane Austen*. London: Routledge & Kegan Paul, 1968; rpt. 1979.

Stern, G.B. and Sheila Kaye-Smith. *Talking of Jane Austen*. London: Cassell, 1943.

——. *More Talk of Jane Austen*. London, 1950.

Van Ghent, Dorothy. *The English Novel: Form and Function*. New York, 1953.

Warner, S.T. "Jane Austen," in *Writers and Their Works* Series. Longmans for the British Council, 1951; rev. ed. 1964.

Watt, Ian. Ed. *Jane Austen: Twentieth Century Views*. Spectrum Books. Engle-wood Cliffs, N.J.: Prentice Hall Inc., 1963.

Whitty, Carole. *Jane Austen: Pride and Prejudice*. London: Harap, 1974.

Woolf, Virginia. *The Common Reader: First Series*. 1925; rpt. London: The Hogarth Press, 1957.

Wright, A.H. *Jane Austen's Novels: A Study in Structure*. London: Chatto & Windus, 1953; 2nd ed. 1962.

A Brief Glossary

(Jane Austen employs some terms which are so little used now, or have altered their meanings so much, that some clarification is required to save the unwary readers from any misapprehension of the text.)

Ablution : washing

Accost : address

Acrimony : bitterness

Address : manner

Addresses : courtship

Adieus : words at parting

Apothecary : an adviser on the use of remedies for minor illness; not a regular doctor.

Application : request

Arch : innocently roguish

Article : contract

Asperity : sharpness

Assembly : ball

At all events : at all costs

Backgamnon : a game played on a special board with pieces moved according to the throw of the dice

Backwards : in the back

Bandbox : a high cardboard box for keeping fashionable hats of women

Barefaced : direct

Barouche	:	a four-wheeled carriage with cover that can be opened in fine weather
Barouche box	:	the seat outside, beside the driver, in a barouche
Beaux	:	admirers
Bequest	:	legacy
Blowsy	:	untidy
Boulanger	:	a kind of dance
Candid	:	specifically free from malice
Canvass	:	discuss
Capital	:	the best
Caprice	:	unaccountable change
Cassino	:	a card game for four players
Chagrin	:	disappointment
Chaise	:	an open carriage
Chaperon	:	to be in charge of a young unmarried woman during social occasions
Chief of everyday	:	major part of each day
Chief of the night	:	greater part of the night
Commerce	:	a popular card game of the rummy type
Complaisance	:	friendliness, politeness
Connection	:	relation by marriage
Conubial	:	married
Contrariwise	:	on the other hand
Controvert	:	dispute
Conversible	:	able to be talked to
Countenance	:	encourage, expression, support
Counterpart	:	equal
Country	:	county
Covies	:	broods of patridges
Crossed in love	:	unfortunate in love
Curricle	:	a light two-wheeled carriage

Debts of honour	:	debts incurred in games of chance, not recoverable by law
Decamping	:	running away
Deck	:	cover
Develop	:	understand, discover, make known
Dissipation	:	frivolous amusement, wasteful spending
Diverted	:	entertained, amused
Draught	:	medicine
Easy circumstances	:	a fairly good income
Eclat	:	conspicuous success
Eminence	:	hill
Encumberance	:	annoyance
Engage	:	promise
Enormity	:	wickedness
Ensigncy	:	the rank of an ensign, the lowest rank of an officer who carried the regimental colours on the flag
Entail	:	settlement of inheritance to a line of heirs so that none of them can give it away or sell it. In England, in Jane Austen's time, in the absence of a male heir in the family, the property used to pass on to the closest male relative of the family.
Equipage	:	carriage with horses and servants
Exigence	:	emergency
Expostulation	:	remonstration
Express	:	telegram
First circles	:	highest rank
Fish	:	a counter made of bone or ivory to keep count in games
Fishing tackle	:	hooks, lines, rods, etc. used for fishing
Fix	:	attach

Fordyce's sermons	:	a book of sermons written by Reverend James Fordyce (1720-96), a popular preacher
Gamester	:	gambler
Gaming debts	:	debts arising out of card games played for money
Gig	:	a two-wheeled carriage drawn by one horse
Going forward	:	happening
Gratification	:	pleasure
Hackney-coach	:	*horse-drawn carriage for hire*
Hauteur	:	haughtiness
High diversion	:	great amusement
Home questions	:	questions of a very personal nature
Implacable	:	unappeasable
Impolitic	:	unsuitable, unwise
Improved	:	cultivated
Ingenuity	:	skilful planning
Iniquitous	:	wicked, unjust
Intelligence	:	news
Intelligible	:	literally audible
La!	:	old fashioned form of 'Oh'
Laconic	:	brief
Livery	:	uniform worn by servants in a large house to be identified as servants of a particular house
Living	:	salaried post given to a clergyman often under the control of the local landowner
Lodge	:	a small cottage by the gate of the park, attached to the main building of a large estate, intended for the gate-keepers
Loo	:	a popular card game
Lottery tickets	:	game of chance

Michaelmas	:	the feast day of St. Michael observed on 29 September every year
Muffin	:	a quick bread made in a small cup-shaped mould, and eaten hot
Overset	:	upset
Overture	:	offer
Paddock	:	a grassy plot in front of house; a grassy field for keeping or exercising horses
Paling	:	wooden fence made of pales or pointed pieces of wood
Peculiar	:	particular
Person	:	body, as opposed to mind
Perverseness	:	error
Phaeton	:	a four-wheeled open carriage drawn by two horses
Pin money	:	money given by a husband to his wife for her own expenses
Piqued	:	prided (oneself)
Piquet	:	a card game for two
Playing high	:	playing with high stakes; risking large sums of money
Pool of quadrille	:	the required number of players for the card game of quadrille
Portion	:	money given to a daughter on her marriage
Position	:	contention
Post	:	hired
Postilion	:	person who rides on one of the horses drawing a carriage when there is no driver
Powdering gown	:	a special thin gown to protect clothes when white powder was being applied to the hair for fashion
Precipitance	:	hurried action
Preferment	:	promotion

Pretension	:	claim
Probity	:	honesty
Punch	:	drink made with wine and spices
Quadrille	:	a kind of card game, also a kind of dance in which four couples are required
Quartered	:	camped
Ragout	:	spiced meat and vegetable stew
Rapacity	:	keenness
Rectitude	:	rightness
Reel	:	a vigorous Scottish dance
Regimentals	:	a soldier's uniform showing his rank
Rencontre	:	meeting, encounter
Saucy	:	cheeky
Scruple	:	hesitate
Seminaries	:	places of education similar to a present day finishing school
Se'nnight	:	week
Self-consequence	:	self-importance
Set	:	group of dancers arranged for dancing in a fixed pattern, each group of four or more making a set in two lines or in a square or a circle
Settlements	:	legal provision in marriage regarding how much dowry the bride would bring and how much money the groom would settle on his wife
Sharp	:	clever in avoiding expense
Shoe-roses	:	ornaments worn on ladies' dancing shoes
Simper	:	smile artificially
Smirk	:	smile stupidly
Solicitude	:	worry
Spar	:	kinds of crystalline mineral

Special licence	:	permission to marriage in special circumstances
Sphere	:	social class
Spleen	:	spite
Suit	:	offer of marriage
St James	:	the court of the ruling King or Queen of England
Stoutly	:	courageously
Teazing	:	persuading jokingly with a serious intention
Tenor	:	tone
Tete a tete	:	private conversation
Threadbare	:	well-worn
Tractable	:	easily handled
Transports	:	strong emotions
Turnpike	:	toll-gate where vehicles are stopped to collect fees for the use of the road
Tythe	:	one-tenth of the annual produce from the land paid as tax to the clergy by the parishioners
Unassailed	:	unspoiled
Unshackle	:	untie
Unstudied	:	unintentional
Untinctured	:	uncoloured
Vingt-un	:	a popular card game more commonly known as pontoon
Vestibule	:	entrance hall, lobby
Vouchsafe	:	condescend
Whist	:	a card game for four players
Young olive branch	:	an offspring, a child

Index

A Memoir of Jane Austen, 4
Addison, ix, 140
Allen, Walter, ix, 142, 146, 148
American Revolution, 1
As You Like It, 87
Aristotle, 86
Austen-Leigh, J.E., 4
Baker, 86
Bakhtinian, 93
Bath, x, 2
Bigg-Wither, Harris, 2
Bowen, Elizabeth, 147
Bradley, Dr, 110, 133, 145
Brontë, Charlotte, 144-45
Brower, Reuben Arthur, 141, 147
Burney, Fanny, ix, 2, 65, 140
Byron, Lord, ix
Cecilia, 65
Chapman, R.W., 145-46
Chaucer, 80
Coleridge, 140
Comedy of Manners, 87
Congreve, xi
Cornish, F.W., 65
Cowper, 2
Crabbe, 2
Daiches, David, 75, 146
Dickens, 95, 133
Edgeworth, Maria, 2
Elinor and Marianne, 3
Emma, 4, 146
Fielding, Henry, xi, 91, 130, 140
First Impressions, 3, 65
FitzGerald, Edward, 145
Forster, E.M., 91, 145, 147
French Revolution, ix
Freud, 146
Garrod, H.W., 145
Goldsmith, ix, 140
Gretna Green, 13, 52
Hardy, Thomas, vii
Johnson, Dr, ix, 2, 130
Johnsonese, 96
Kaye-Smith, Sheila, 147
Kennedy, Mrs Margaret, 81
Kettle, Arnold, 137
Knight, Fanny, 75
Lady Susan, 3-4
Lake Poets, 69
Lamb, 80
Leavis, F.R., 140
Love and Friendship, 3
Lubbock, 91
Macaulay, 94, 140

Mansfield, Katherine, 145, 147
Mansfield Park, 4, 146
Marx, 75, 146
Metcalfe, Lady, 11
Mozart, 141
Much Ado About Nothing, 87
Mudrick, Professor, 84
Muir, Edwin, 145
Napoleonic Wars, vii
Northanger Abbey, 4
Oedipus Complex, 146
Persuasion, 4
Pierce, F.E., viii
Pope, ix
Radcliffe, Mrs Ann, ix, 2, 140
Rebellion in Ireland, vii
Richardson, 2, 3, 89
Sandition, 4
Schorer, Mark, 74, 146
Scott, Sir Walter, ix, 4, 76, 133, 144
Sense and Sensibility, 3, 146
Shakespeare, 80, 87, 94, 142
Shelley, ix
Smollett, 130
Sophocles, 86
Southey, Robert, 4
Sterne, ix, 140
Sterne G.B., 147
Terpsichorean, 2
Thackeray, 133
The Watsons, 3-4, 79
War, vii
Wordsworth, ix, 140, 144
Woolf, Virginia, 145, 147
Wright, A.H., 68, 84